Exotic Pentatonic Soloing

Published by www.fundamental-chang

ISBN: 978-1-910403-30-3

Copyright © 2015 Simon Pratt

The moral right of this author has been asserted.

All rights reserved. No part of this publication may be reproduced, stored in a retrieval system, or transmitted in any form or by any means, without the prior permission in writing from the publisher. The publisher is not responsible for websites (or their content) that are not owned by the publisher.

www.fundamental-changes.com

Backing Tracks Provided By Jacob **Quist** Quistgaard

Audio available from

www.fundamental-changes.com/download-audio

Video available from:

www.fundamental-changes.com/exotic-pentatonic-soloing

Front Cover Image © CanStockPhoto / carloscastilla

Other Books by Fundamental Changes

Rock Rhythm Guitar Playing

Heavy Metal Rhythm Guitar

Heavy Metal Lead Guitar Book 1

Heavy Metal Lead Guitar Book 2

The Practical Guide to Modern Music Theory for Guitarists

Rock Guitar Un-CAGED: The CAGED System and 100 Licks for Rock Guitar

Guitar Fretboard Fluency

Guitar Scales in Context

Complete Technique for Modern Guitar

The CAGED System and 100 Licks for Blues Guitar

The Complete Guide to Playing Blues Guitar Book One: Rhythm Guitar

The Complete Guide to Playing Blues Guitar Book Two: Melodic Phrasing

The Complete Guide to Playing Blues Guitar Book Three: Beyond Pentatonics

The Complete Guide to Playing Blues Guitar Compilation

Fundamental Changes in Jazz Guitar: The Major ii V I

Minor ii V Mastery for Jazz Guitar

Jazz Blues Soloing for Guitar

Guitar Chords in Context Part One

Jazz Guitar Chord Mastery (Guitar Chords in Context Part Two)

Funk Guitar Mastery

The Complete Technique, Theory and Scales Compilation for Guitar

Sight Reading Mastery for Guitar

Beginner's Guitar Lessons: The Essential Guide

Chord Tone Soloing for Jazz Guitar

Contents

Introduction 4

Chapter One: Maximise Your Practice 5

Chapter Two: Introduction to the CAGED System 10

    Intervals and Scale Formulas 13

Chapter Three: The Minor Pentatonic Scale 14

Chapter Four: The Major Pentatonic Scale 22

Chapter Five: The 'Hindu' Pentatonic Scale 28

Chapter Six: The Blues Pentatonic Scale 34

Chapter Seven: The Robben Ford Pentatonic Scale 40

Chapter Eight: The 'No Root add9' Pentatonic Scale 45

Chapter Nine: The Lydian Pentatonic Scale 51

Chapter Ten: The m7b5 Pentatonic Scale 57

Chapter Eleven: The Maj7#5 Pentatonic Scale 63

Chapter Twelve: The Iwato Pentatonic Scale 68

Chapter Thirteen: The Hirojoshi Pentatonic Scale 74

Chapter Fourteen: Improvising 80

Chapter Fifteen: Building Melodic Phrases 82

Chapter Sixteen: Minor Pentatonic Substitution 85

Chapter Seventeen: Developing your Sound 88

Conclusion 91

Recommended Listening 92

Other Books from Fundamental Changes 93

Introduction

Welcome to Exotic Pentatonic Soloing for Guitar!

Pentatonic scales contain five notes and they are a ticket to creative, expressive soloing. In this book, we will look at how to use different types of pentatonic scales in blues, rock, jazz, pop and funk music.

The starting point is the Minor Pentatonic scale as it is the 'bread and butter' approach for most modern guitarists. From there, we investigate ten other types of pentatonic scales, covering different shapes and patterns that will inspire you to make more creative music. The guitar allows complete freedom of expression and these pentatonic scales form a palette of colours to enhance your art.

Each scale is given in the five different CAGED shapes, with full tablature and five useful licks allowing you to link up the fretboard.

Exotic Pentatonic Soloing also includes private video lessons, as well as audio tracks to download for every example in the book.

You can download the audio from www.fundamental-changes.com/download-audio

The videos are available from

www.fundamental-changes.com/exotic-pentatonic-soloing

The password for these videos is given in chapter one.

Good luck and have fun!

Simon

Jacob 'Quist' Quistgaard has professionally recorded the backing tracks in this book. Check out his website for some excellent resources.

http://www.quistorama.com

Chapter One: Maximise Your Practice

Video: www.fundamental-changes.com/exotic-pentatonic-soloing

The password to this video is given at the end of this chapter

Before launching into the eleven different types of pentatonic scale, this chapter looks at how you can get the most out of your practice. I call the following exercises 'ultimate lick builders'. With these exercises, you will gain the maximum value from every new scale that you learn.

The following examples use the A Minor Pentatonic scale, but you should apply these ideas to other keys.

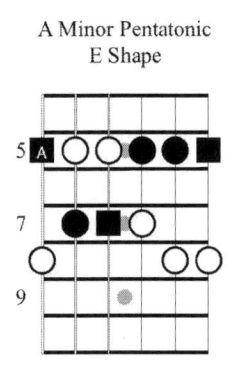

A Minor Pentatonic
E Shape

The square dots indicated in this diagram show the root notes of the scale (in this case 'A'), and the circular notes outline the other scale tones. The solid black dots highlight the chord shape that the scale is built around, in this case Am.

Example 1a: (Down and up through the scale shape)

This exercise is a basic way to practice scales. The aim is to ascend and descend across all six strings.

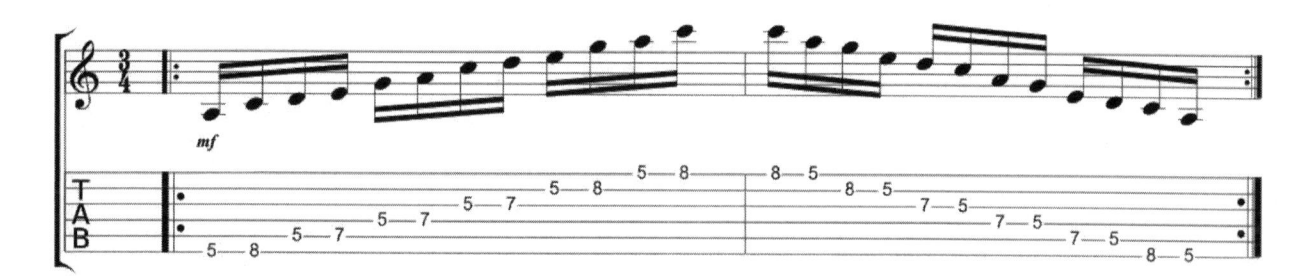

Another way to practice scales is to combine groups of notes into patterns of threes, fours, fives or sixes.

Example 1b: (Three-note groupings)

Example 1c: (Four-note groupings)

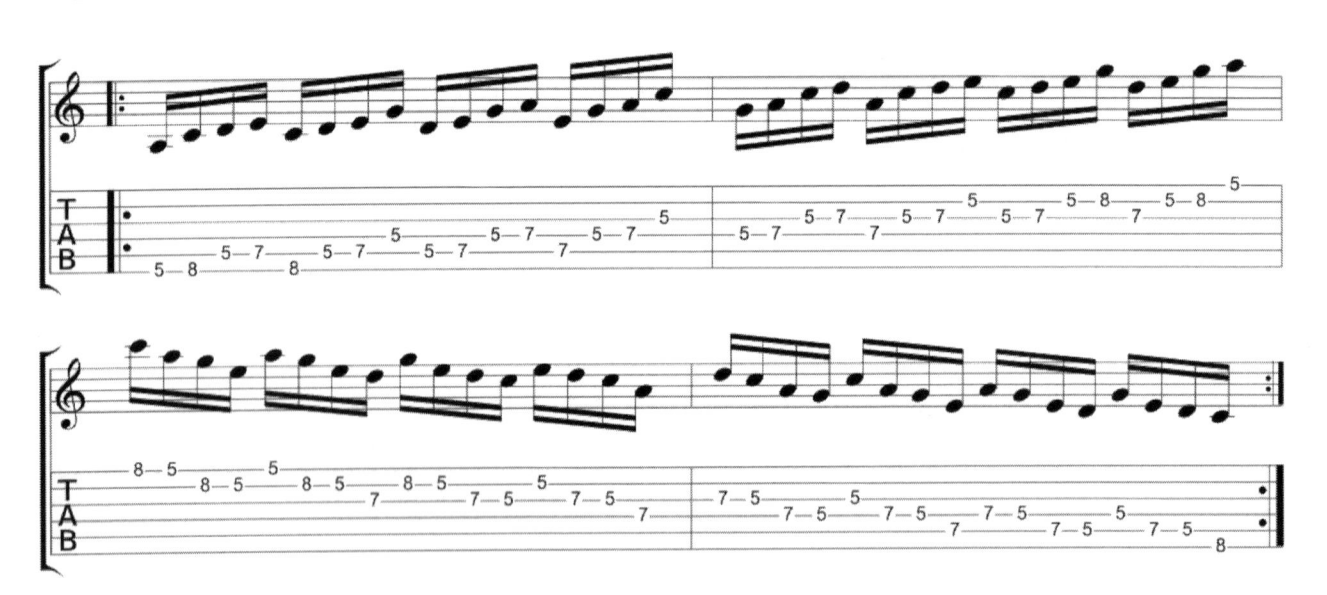

Example 1d: (Five-note groupings)

Example 1e: (Six-note groupings)

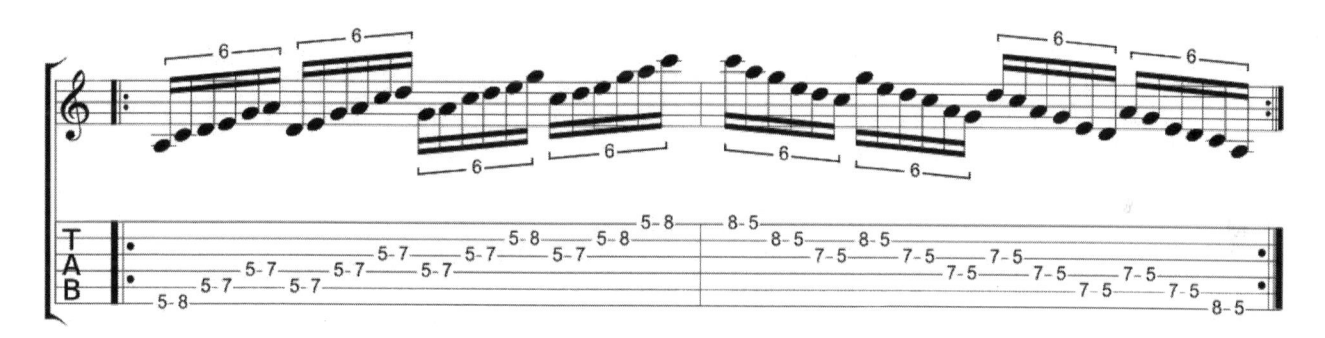

In music, an *interval* is the name for the distance between two notes.

To move away from playing sequential scale steps we can use intervals to add musical jumps By using bigger intervals in solos, we can create exciting ideas that break away from predictable, linear scale runs.

In example 1f, we break the Minor Pentatonic scale into intervals of a *4th*.

Example 1f: (Practicing scales in intervals)

In the next example, we join together the five positions of the A Minor Pentatonic scale. This is a useful way to map out the whole fretboard and create longer licks and lines.

Example 1g: (Five positions together)

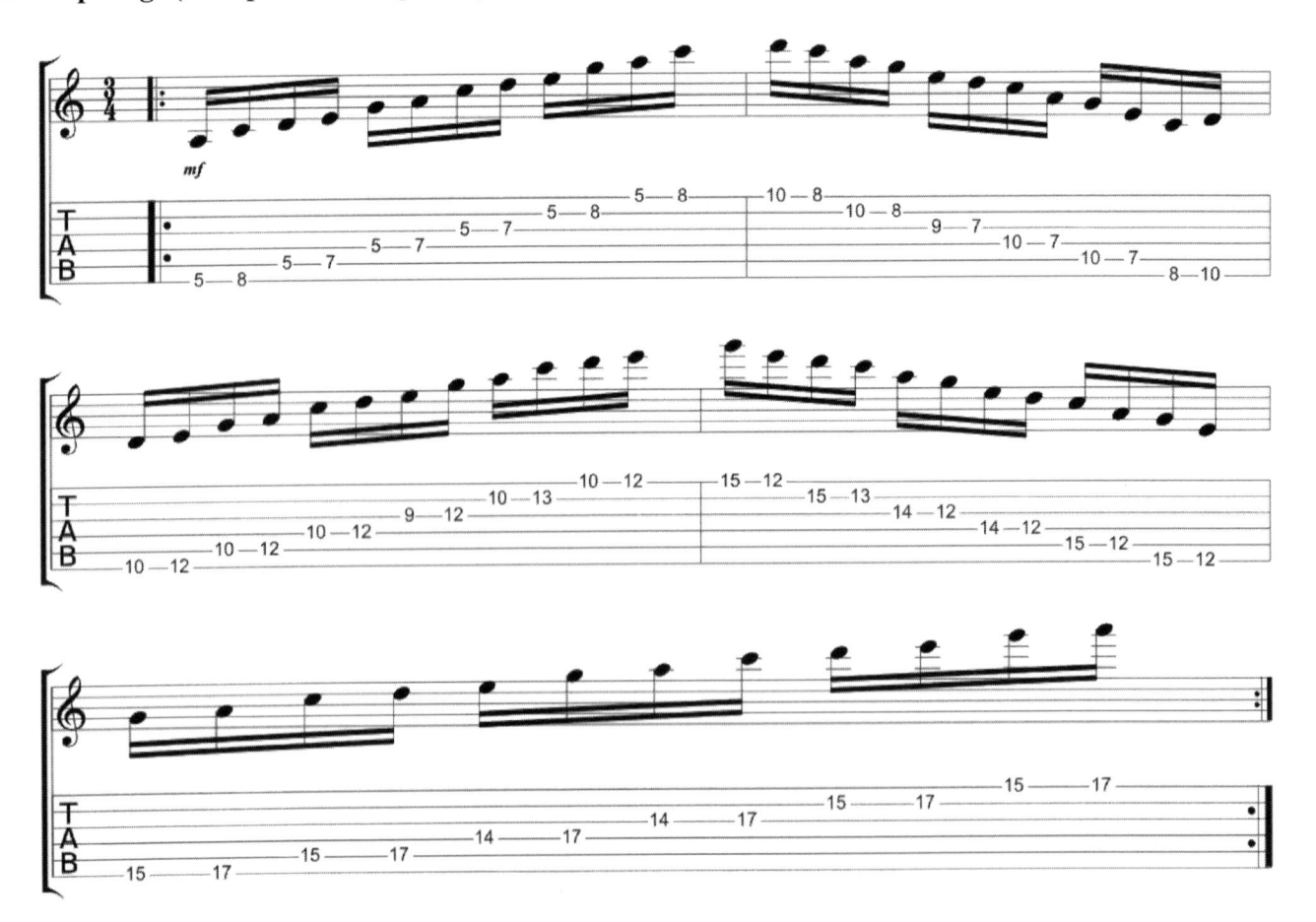

It is also possible to take a piano-like approach by playing each note along just one string. Practicing in this way breaks us out of any scale/shape ruts we may be stuck in, and helps us to concentrate on the *sound* of the scale we are learning. I often create melodies on one string before finding a more comfortable way to play them.

Example 1h: (Single string, one octave)

Another way to add interest to your licks is to skip strings when playing scale shapes. In this next example, you can see how to create big melodic leaps by introducing string skips.

Example 1i: (String skipping)

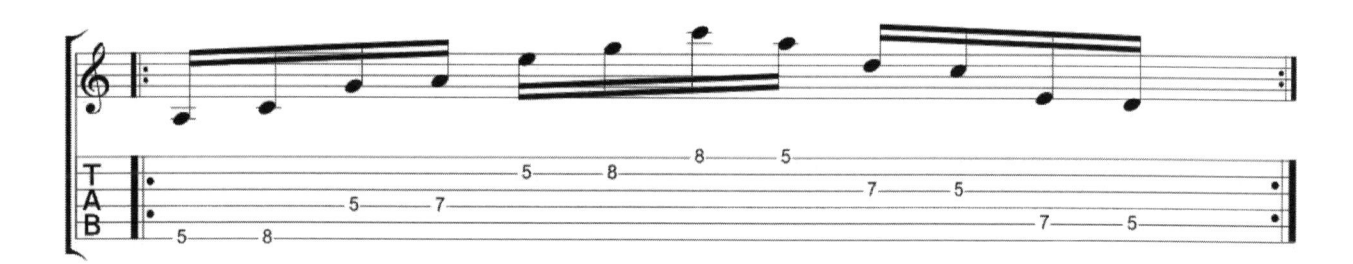

The password to all the videos in this book is **hirojoshi**

Chapter Two: Introduction to the CAGED System

Throughout this book, each scale shape is taught around the CAGED system. In the CAGED system, every chord, scale, and arpeggio shape can be played using five different patterns, allowing guitarists to divide the whole fretboard into five manageable chunks.

The CAGED system was popularised by the jazz guitar virtuoso Joe Pass, but guitarists of all genres now use it as a fretboard navigational tool.

The CAGED system is based on five open chord shapes that you probably already know. Unsurprisingly these are the shapes of C, A G E and D. These shapes are shown below in the key of A Major: The root note (A) is indicated by the square markers.

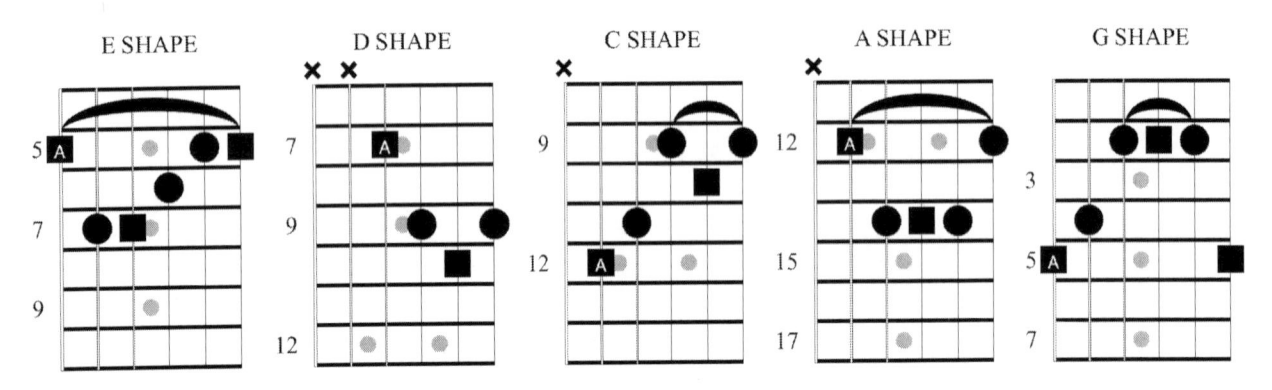

These chord shapes divide the neck into five different sections.

These chord shapes are used as 'anchors' to help us visualise scale shapes that are built around them.

By using visual chord anchors, we are able to quickly build and remember any scale shape we need, and being able to divide the guitar neck into small chunks allows us to solo fluently anywhere on the guitar.

Shown below are the five positions of the A Major Pentatonic scale. You can see how they are built around each chord shape.

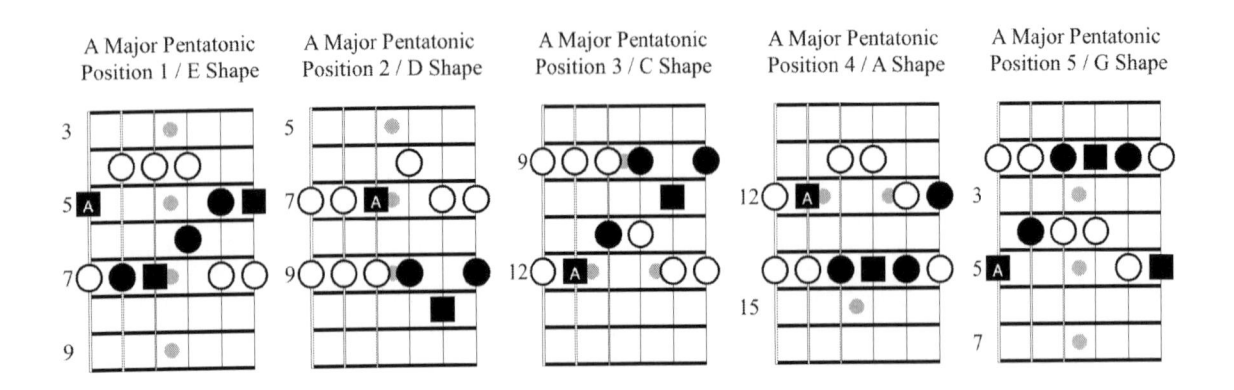

While breaking up the fretboard into small chunks is crucial, being able to see it in its entirety will ultimately lead to more proficient playing.

Shown below are the five CAGED shape A major chords combined together in one diagram.

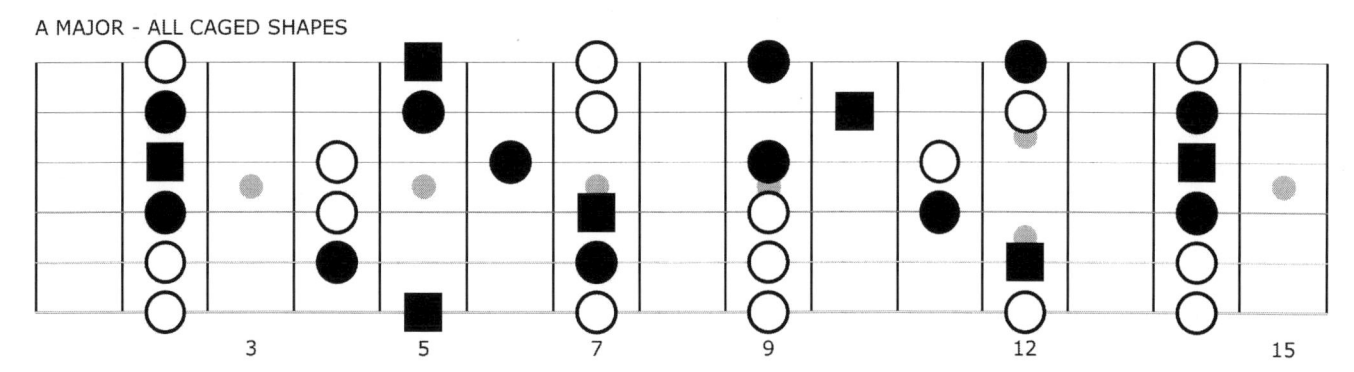

A MAJOR - ALL CAGED SHAPES

See how the A Major Pentatonic scale shapes fit around each of the chord shapes. Chord shapes are more memorable than scale shapes, so it helps to learn them first and then build the scales around them.

The key points to remember with the CAGED system are:

- Five different shapes of the same scale are built around five individual chord shapes
- Building scales around chord shapes make scales easier to memorise and transpose

Throughout the book, you will learn to use the CAGED chord shapes to map out each scale. Shown above are the A *Major* CAGED shapes, which work as the underlying chord shapes for any *Major Pentatonic* scales and licks. These will be addressed in more detail in Chapter Four.

When we use *Minor* Pentatonic scales, we use *minor* chord shapes in the CAGED system.

The Minor CAGED shapes

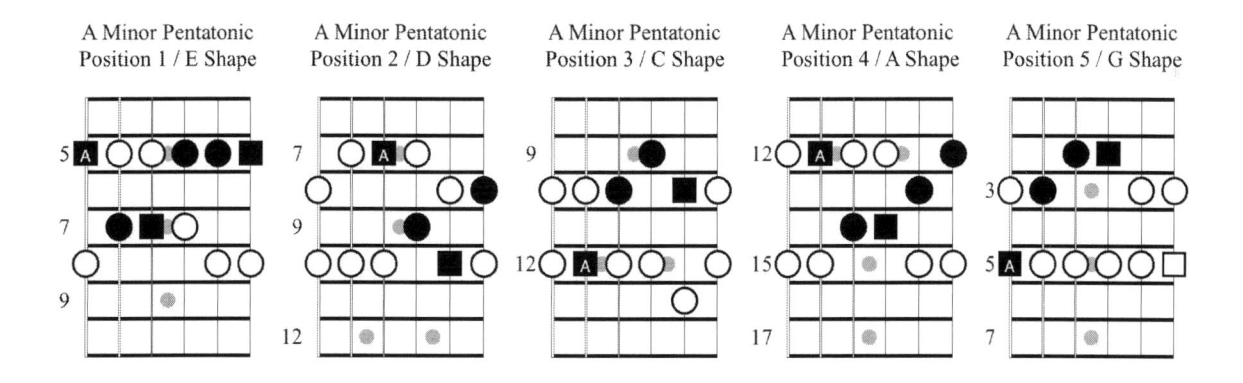

A Minor Pentatonic Position 1 / E Shape
A Minor Pentatonic Position 2 / D Shape
A Minor Pentatonic Position 3 / C Shape
A Minor Pentatonic Position 4 / A Shape
A Minor Pentatonic Position 5 / G Shape

When playing the five Minor Pentatonic scales, learn to see the corresponding chords that lie within them. The dark notes in each scale diagram show the chord that each scale shape is built around.

In the diagram below, all five A minor CAGED scale shapes are laid out across the guitar. This acts as a road map and helps you to solo confidently anywhere on the neck.

The square dots once again show you the root notes of each chord. Analyse how each chord attaches itself to the Minor Pentatonic scales shown above.

11

A MINOR - ALL CAGED

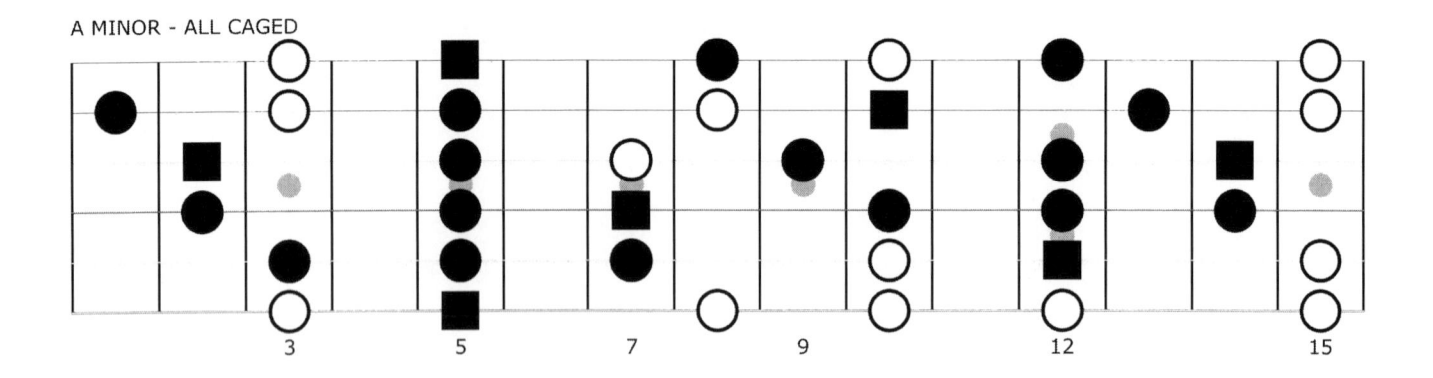

In the Minor Pentatonic chapter of this book, we will explore five different licks created with the scales shown above.

This book takes you through eleven very different types of pentatonic scale. Throughout, you will learn licks built around each of the five chord shapes.

Intervals and Scale Formulas

To highlight and define the differences in scales, musicians compare the structure (step pattern) of a scale to structure of the Major scale. The Major scale is the building block of most music, so it is considered a good 'base' to use as a reference.

The distance (interval) from one note to the next defines a scale's structure, for example, C to D, D to E, E to F, etc. The distance from C to D is a tone (two frets on the guitar), but the distance from E to F is only a semitone (one fret on the guitar). The structure of any Major scale is always:

Tone, Tone, Semitone, Tone, Tone, Tone, Semitone.

As the Major scale is the building block of most music, its pattern of tones and semitones is given the simple formula 1 2 3 4 5 6 7.

We now have a 'standard' that we can use to help us compare the characteristics of different scales.

Major scales contain seven notes, but pentatonic scales are five-note scales, so their scale formulas only contain five notes.

Every scale in this book is in the key of A. Every pentatonic formula throughout the book will be compared to the A major scale which contains the notes:

A B C# D E F# G#

(1 2 3 4 5 6 7).

Chapter Three: The Minor Pentatonic Scale

Video: www.fundamental-changes.com/exotic-pentatonic-soloing Password: hirojoshi

Backing Track One

The Minor Pentatonic scale is, without a doubt, the most commonly used scale by guitarists. From the playing of Jimi Hendrix to Eric Clapton, and Larry Carlton to Carlos Santana, many of the greatest guitar solos are based around minor pentatonic ideas.

This scale shape is popular because it is accessible, easy to play, and also sounds fantastic! The Minor Pentatonic is at the root of all blues music and therefore is the basis of every genre of modern music that grew from the blues, such as rock, jazz and funk.

The word 'pentatonic' describes the *construction* of the scale. '*Pent*' means five and '*tonic*' means tones. All the scales in this book, therefore, contain five separate tones.

The A Minor Pentatonic contains the notes **A C D E** and **G**.

The formula for the Minor Pentatonic scale is **1 b3 4 5 b7**.

The examples in this chapter are all in the key of A minor, and each lick fits perfectly over an A minor chord or a backing track in A minor such as Backing Track One.

A Minor Pentatonic – Position 1 'E' shape

The barre chord marked by the black dots is the visual cue for this position of the Minor Pentatonic scale. Notice how similar the two shapes are; the Minor Pentatonic scale adds just a few extra notes to the underlying Am chord.

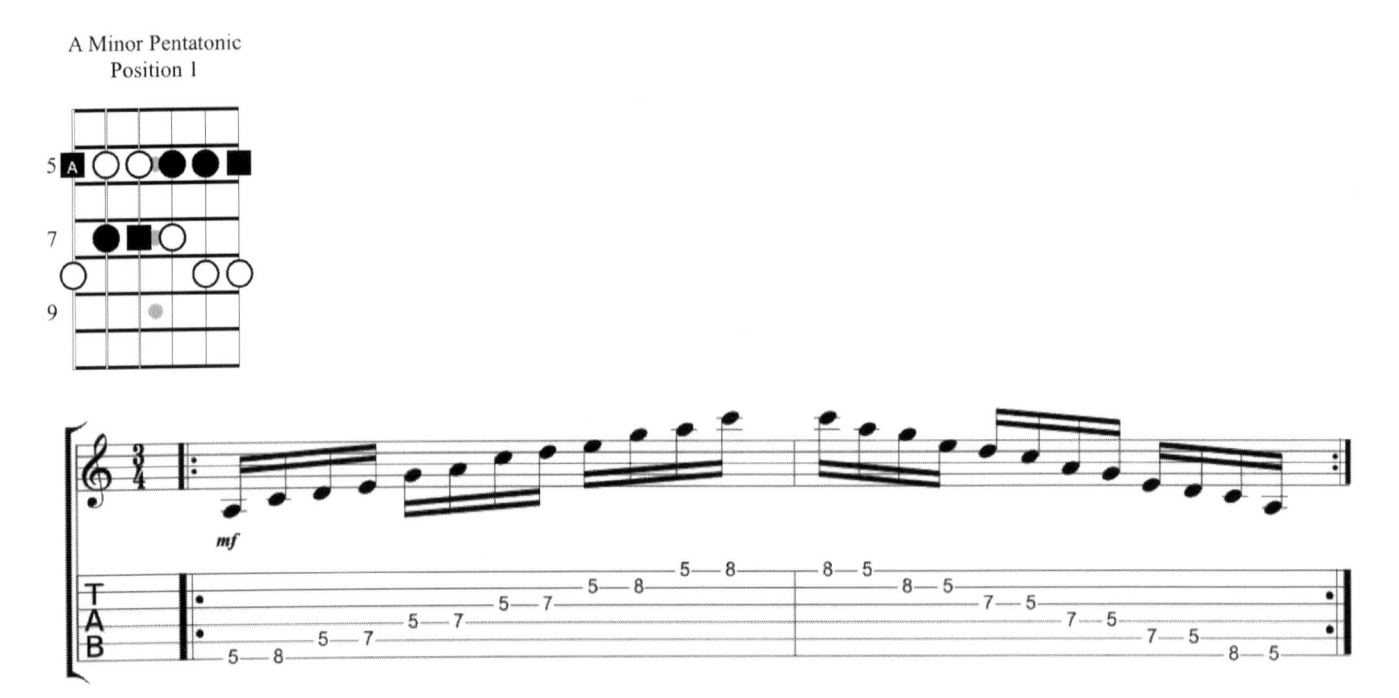

14

The first lick begins with some slow bends and uses vibrato to add expression. Try to keep the bends clean and even, and concentrate on bending in tune.

Aim to make the pull-offs the same volume as the hammer-ons and picked notes, and watch out for unwanted string noise (mute unplayed strings where possible with both hands).

Watch the accompanying video to learn how to add vibrato to this lick. Vibrato will add life and lyrical expression to any musical phrase.

Remember, you can see every a video of every lick played in this book at **www.fundamental-changes.com/exotic-pentatonic-soloing**

You can download the audio at **www.fundamental-changes.com/download-audio.**

Example 3a

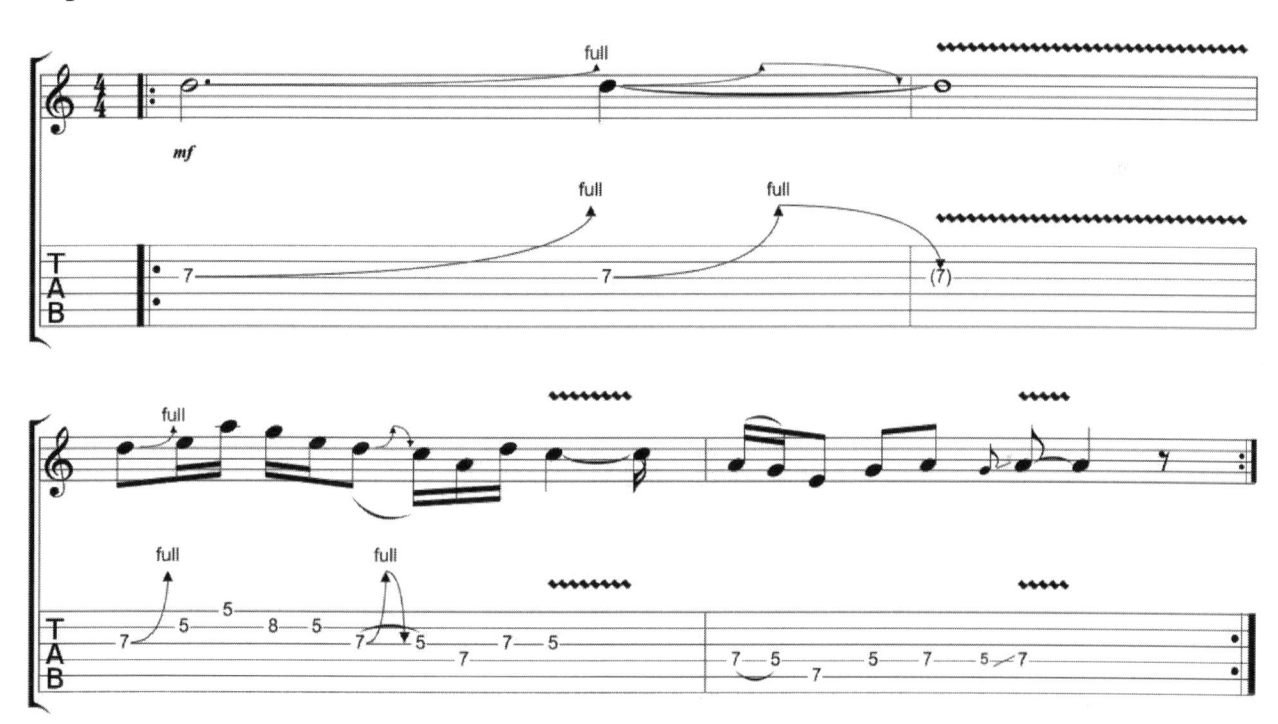

A Minor Pentatonic – Position 2 'D' shape

Next we see position two of both the A minor chord and the A Minor Pentatonic scale. It is important to see the chord shape that lies inside each pentatonic shape.

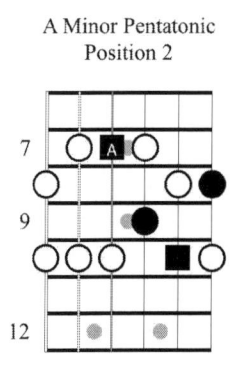

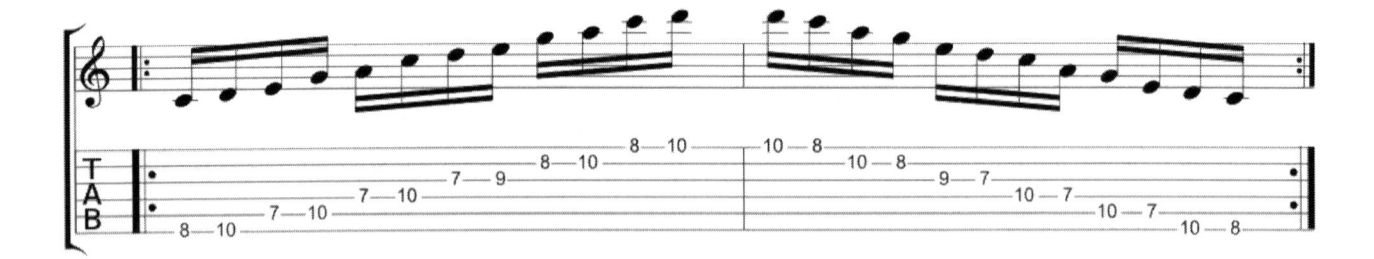

Example 3b begins with a classic blues phrase and combines bends, pull-offs, and vibrato. The double-stops used in bar two add some Hendrix-style phrasing by using a hammer-on to sound a new pitch on the lower string.

Look at the scale diagram shown above and notice where the Hendrix-style double stops are within the shape. Apply this technique to different string sets in this position and create your own Hendrix-style ideas.

Example 3b

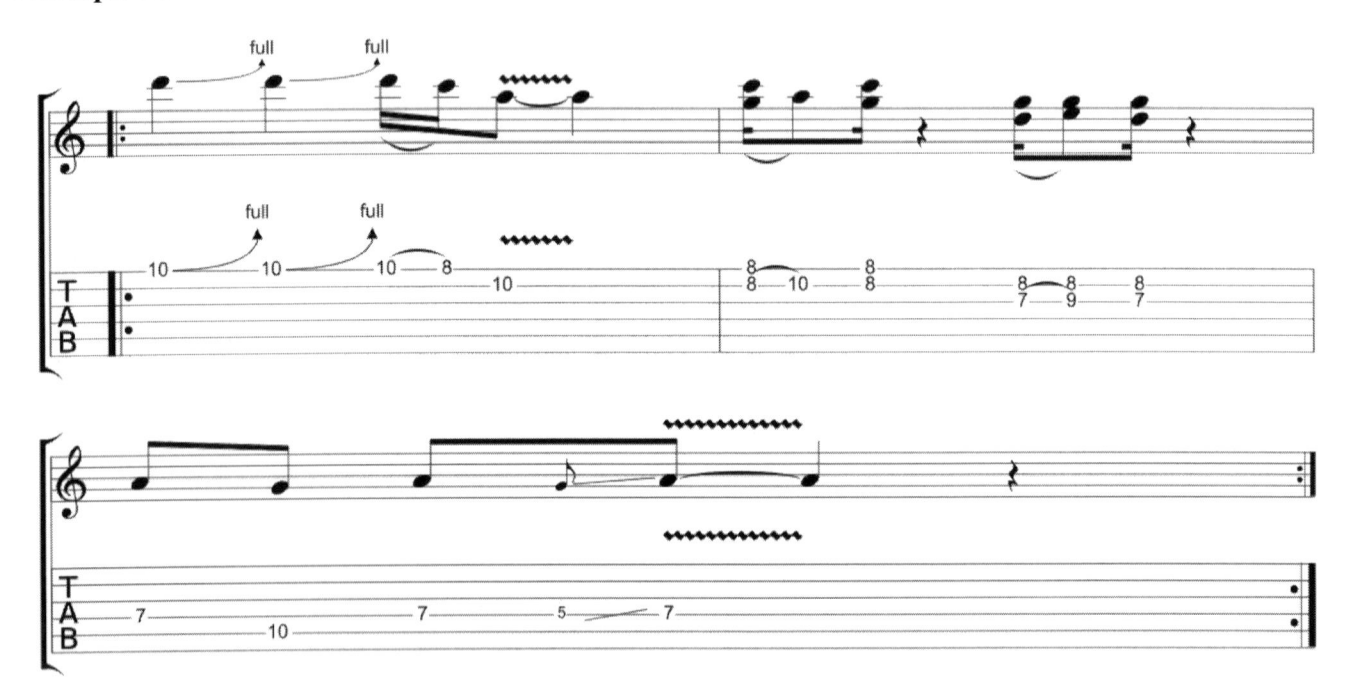

A Minor Pentatonic – Position 3 'C' Shape

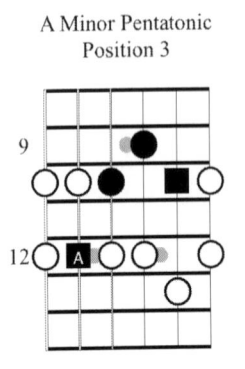

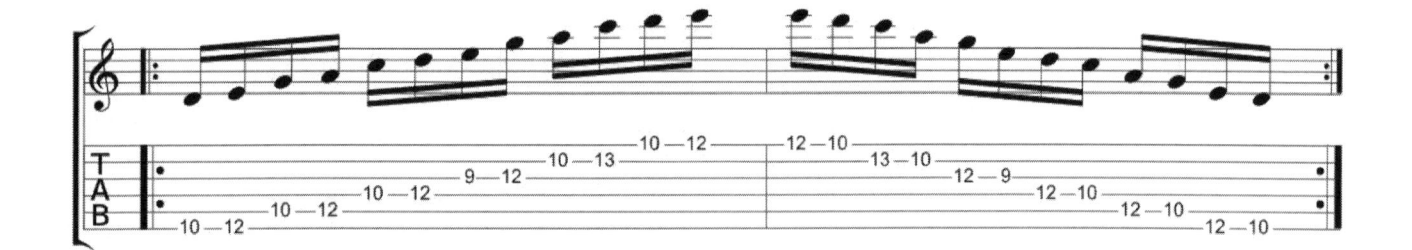

Using hammer-ons and pull-offs allows you to play faster with less effort by halving the number of pick strokes needed. In this example, the repeated rhythmic pattern combined with the *legato* techniques creates a memorable hook. Try this legato pattern with different scale shapes.

Example 3c

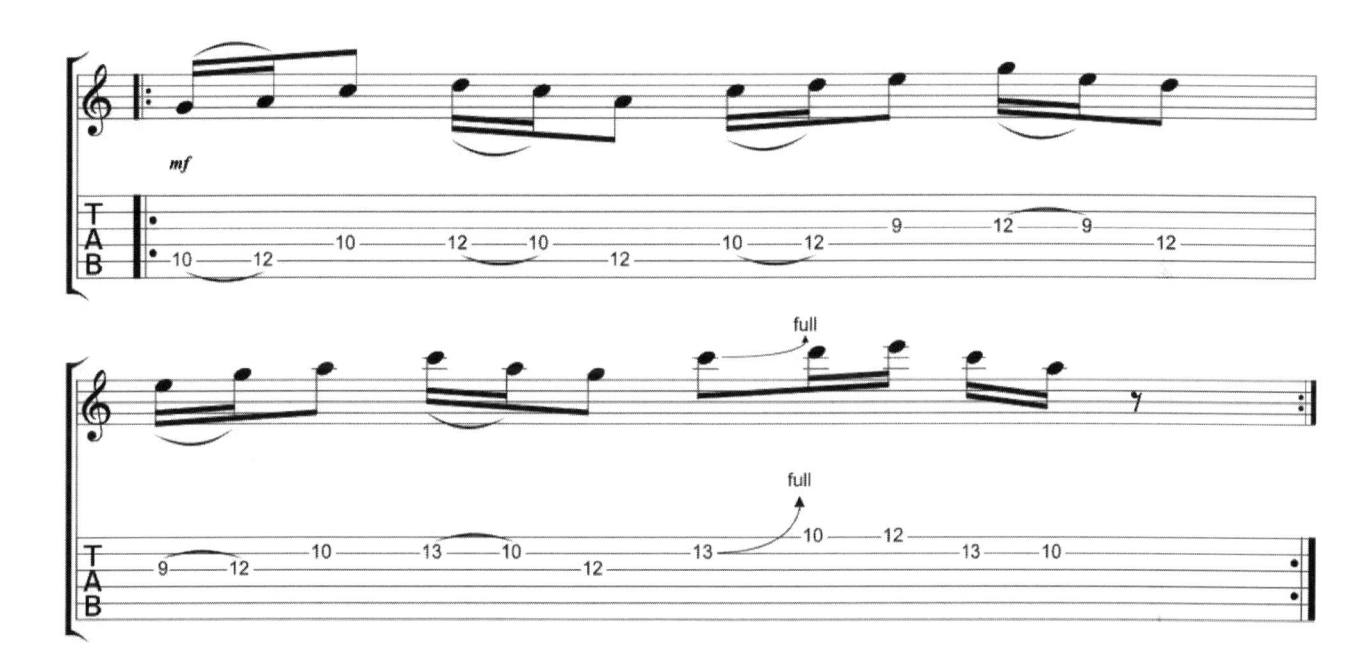

A Minor Pentatonic – Position 4 'A' Shape

Play the chord shape before learning the scale pattern. This helps lock the two together in your mind and will help your fretboard fluency.

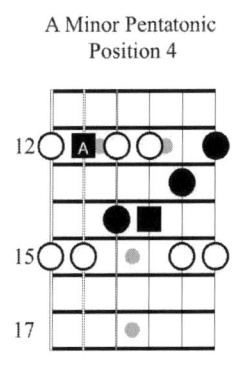

A Minor Pentatonic
Position 4

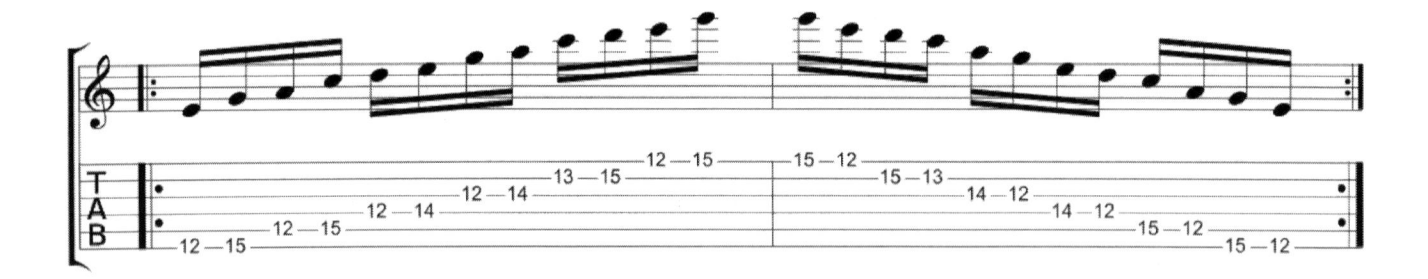

Example 3d demonstrates how you can start a lick at different points in the bar. Adding rests between licks can add excitement and suspense.

When a slide is notated without a specific starting fret, try a two-fret slide in from below. Although a two-fret slide is a good place to begin, starting the slide from further away (above *or* below the target note) can create extremely *vocal-sounding* phrases. Steve Vai uses this technique to great effect in 'For The Love Of God.'

Example 3d

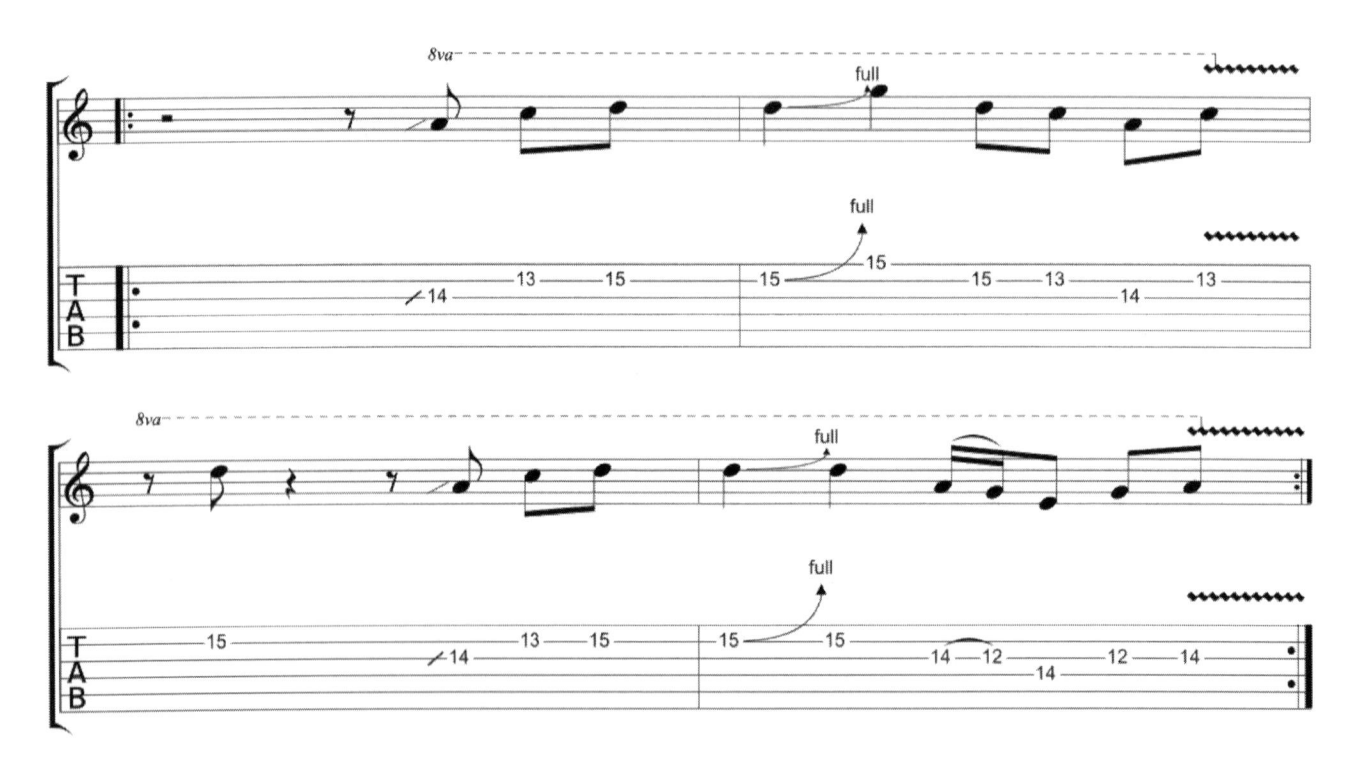

A Minor Pentatonic – Position 5 'G' shape

Once again, use the highlighted chord as an 'anchor' to memorise and navigate the scale.

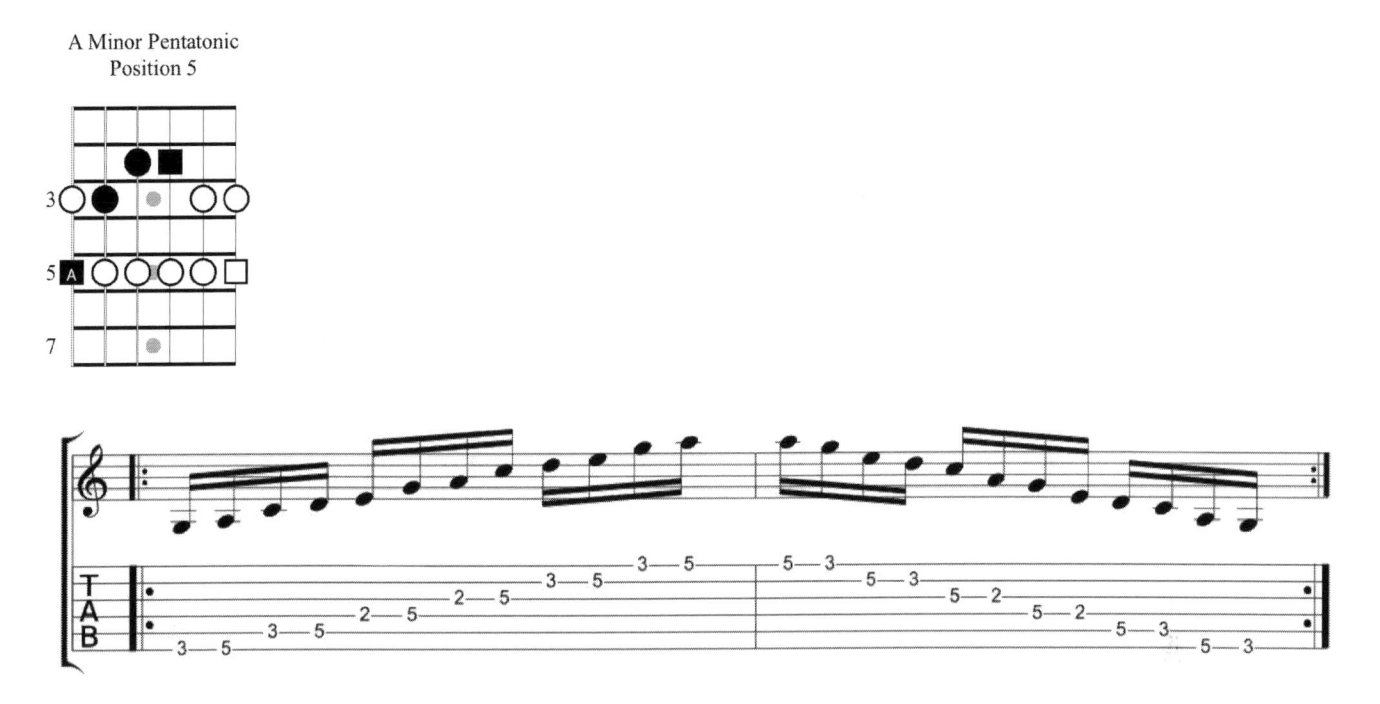

When soloing, the bass (thick) strings are often neglected in favour of the top (thinner) strings, as it is easier to add bends and vibrato to the top strings. Despite the lower strings lending themselves more to riffs than solos, the bass strings have a lot to offer melodically.

Example 3e demonstrates a simple *double-stop* idea with a slide to add excitement. Bar three contains a simple arpeggio idea in A minor.

Example 3e

The Minor Pentatonic scale is just the beginning of your lead guitar playing journey. The licks that are shown in this chapter favour blues and rock, so use 'Backing Track One' as an accompaniment. Once you are comfortable with each lick, put on backing track one and play along. You don't need to worry about copying each note perfectly here; this is the time for you to have fun and to enjoy playing!

A memorable solo combines melodic phrasing, good technique, well-crafted licks and improvisation. To be fluid when improvising it is important to create your own licks as well as copying the licks demonstrated here. A fantastic exercise to improve your improvising is to play a minor pentatonic lick from this chapter, and then improvise for the same length of time it took to play the lick.

Example 3f is a four bar blues-rock lick. Play example 3a then improvise using the A Minor Pentatonic scale for four bars. Include techniques such as bends, hammer-ons, pull-offs, vibrato, and slides when you are improvising. These are fantastic ways to blend the licks you already know with true improvisation while keeping the melody sounding natural.

Stick to alternating between licks you already know and improvisation to stop unwanted 'noodling'. Again, use 'Backing Track One' to practice this idea.

Example 3f with improvisation

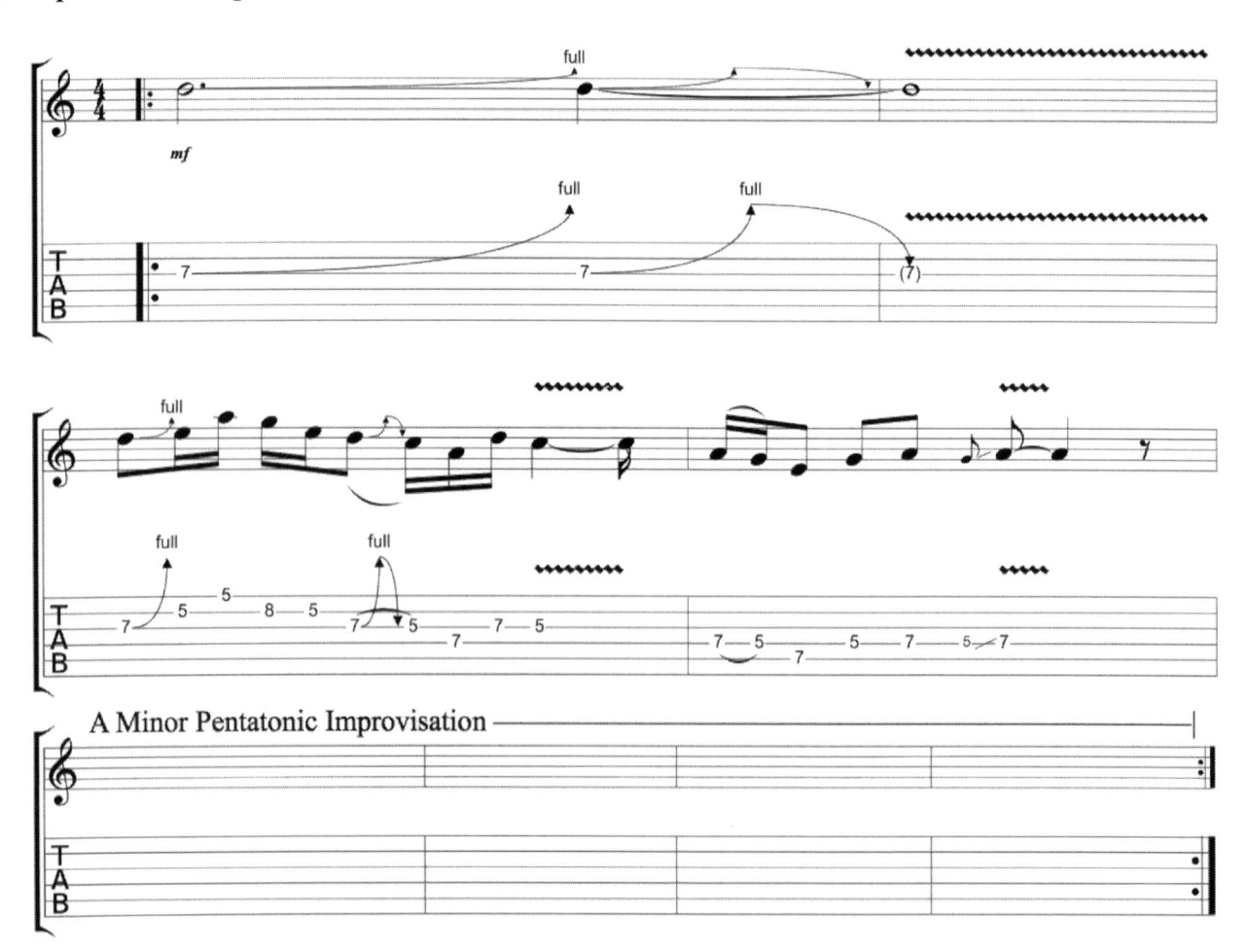

This practice approach reinforces the licks you already know by applying them in a musical setting, but also pushes you to improvise too. It may feel unnatural at first but keep at it as the rewards are worth it.

Remember that while learning scales and licks is crucial to your guitar playing development, it is paramount that you apply them in a variety of musical settings such as playing with a backing track, or jamming with a friend for them to become internalised and natural.

Chapter Four: The Major Pentatonic Scale

Video: www.fundamental-changes.com/exotic-pentatonic-soloing Password: hirojoshi

Backing Track Two

The Major Pentatonic scale sounds happier than its minor counterpart and is synonymous with country, blues and rock although it is very versatile and used in most genres. Slash, Chuck Berry and Eric Clapton are all associated with the Major Pentatonic sound.

The A Major Pentatonic contains the notes **A B C# E F#**.

The formula for the Major Pentatonic scale is 1 2 3 5 6.

In the following examples, each A Major Pentatonic scale shape is shown alongside its accompanying CAGED chord. Make sure you can play the chord and scale before attempting the associated licks.

The licks shown here will work perfectly over any chord progression in A Major.

A Major Pentatonic – Position 1 'E' Shape

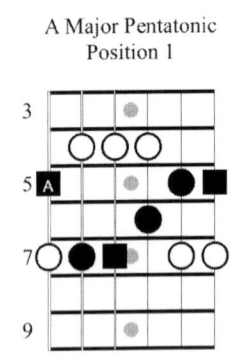

In example 4a, the combination of single notes and double stops shows the versatility of the Major Pentatonic scale. Use the 'one finger per fret' rule throughout this lick to make it easier to play.

Example 4a

A Major Pentatonic – Position 2 'D' Shape

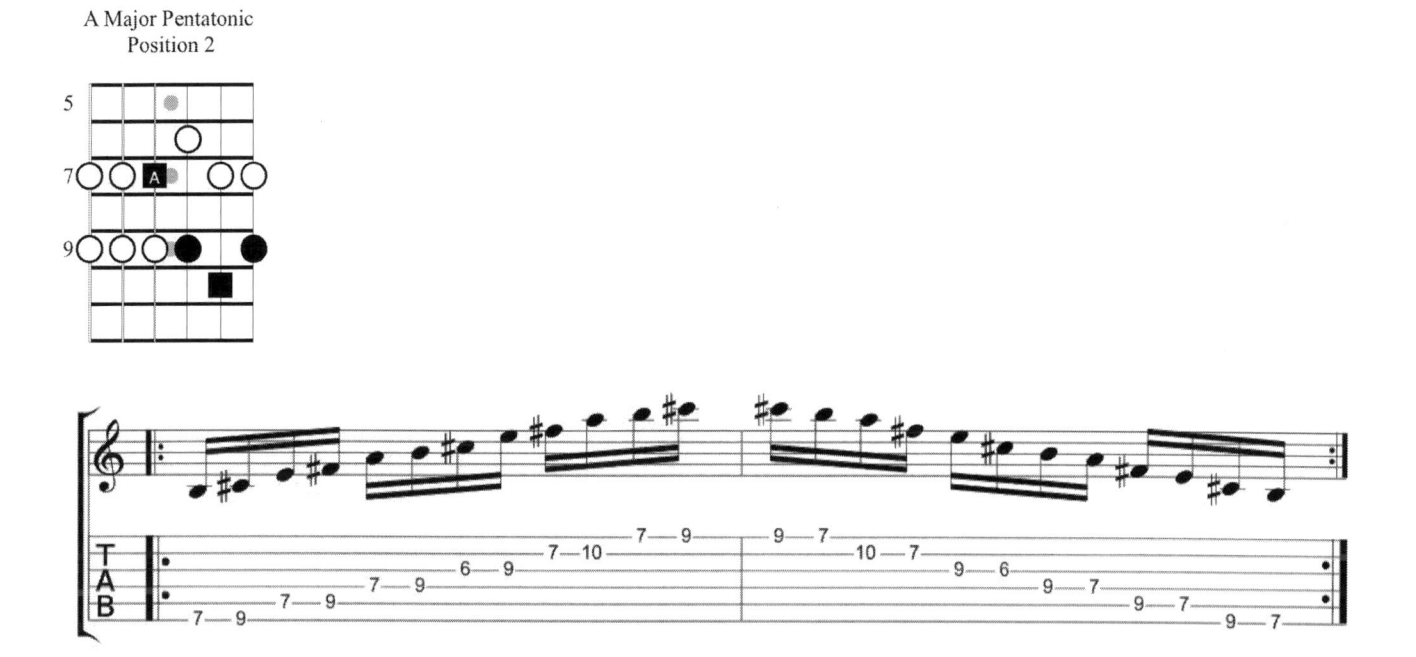

Example 4b combines legato, bends, slides and vibrato, all within two bars. Avoid the temptation play this lick too fast too soon. Build the speed gradually with a metronome, and concentrate on making each note clear.

Example 4b:

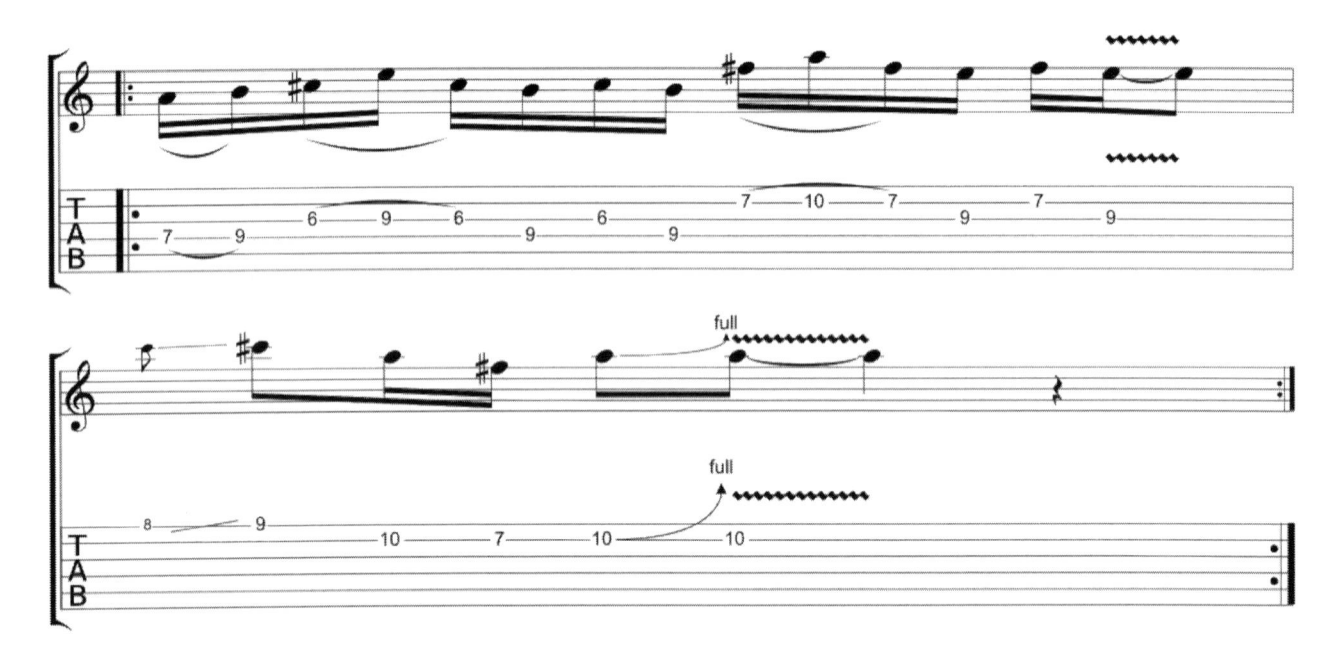

A Major Pentatonic – Position 3 'C' Shape

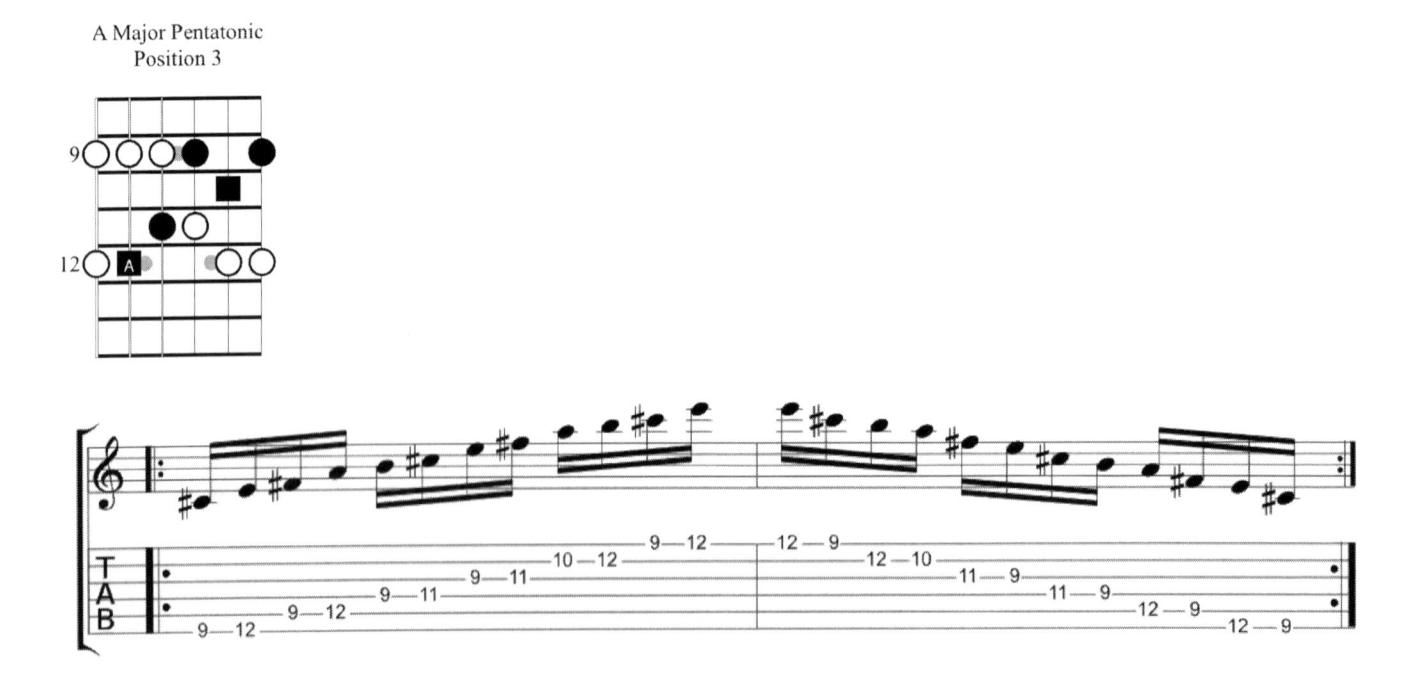

Bends and slides add a vocal quality to lead lines. This next lick is reminiscent of blues players such as John Mayer and is a good example of how 'less can be more', as it uses just a small group of notes.

A great tip is to sing a lick before playing it on the guitar. I first came across this idea when I watched George Benson sing and play his licks at the same time.

Never be afraid to copy and steal as many different ideas from as many guitarists and other musicians as you can. That way, you emulate all the bits you enjoy and bring them into your playing.

Example 4c:

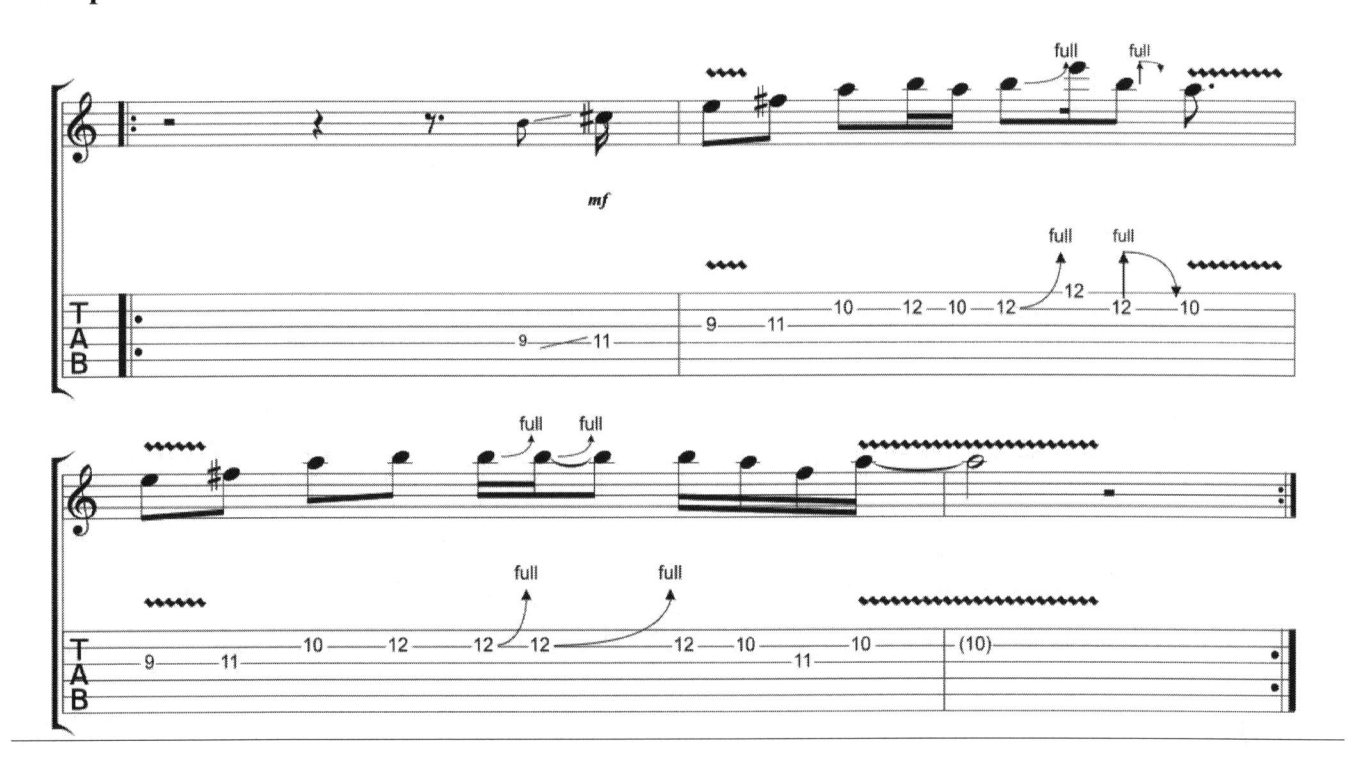

A Major Pentatonic – Position 4 'A' Shape

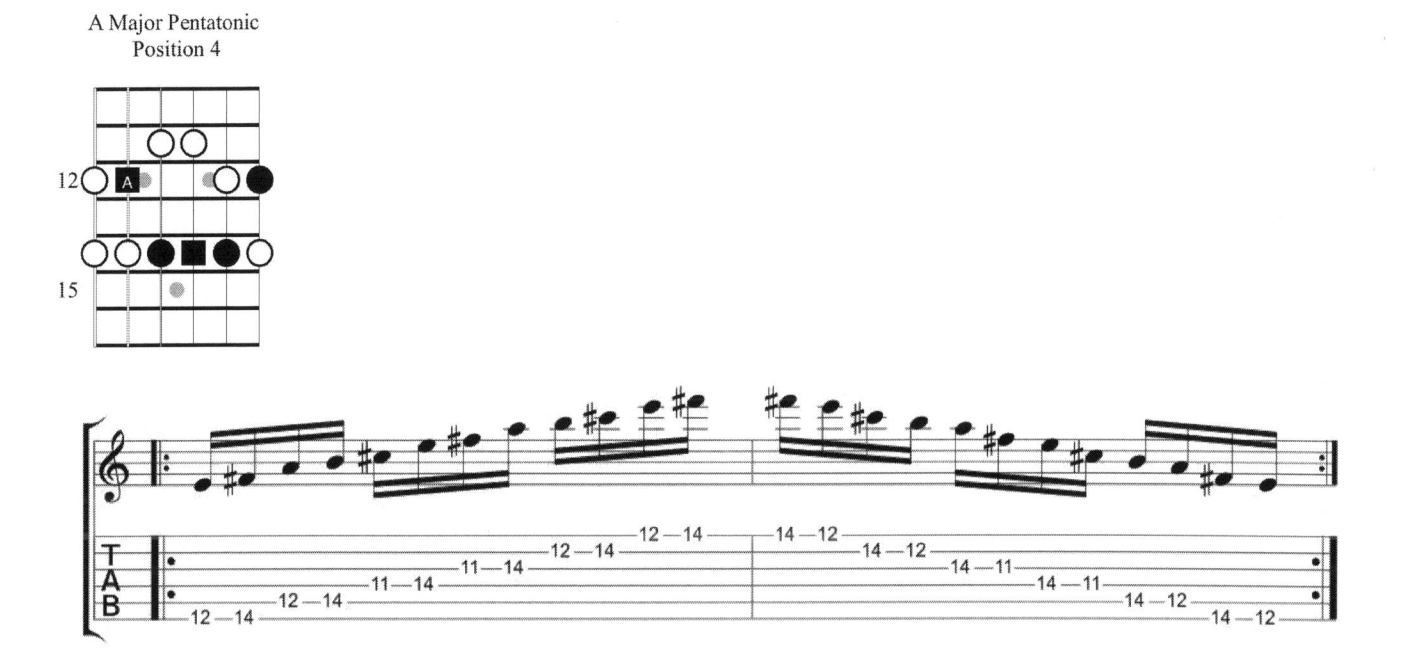

Example 4d has a distinctive Eric Johnson flavour due to its driving 1/16th note phrasing. The first two bars contain alternate-picked notes with subtle vibrato. Make sure you watch me play this lick on video if you are in any doubt about how to finger this idea.

You can incorporate this rhythmic pattern into the other four Major Pentatonic scale shapes and build longer licks that move through each position.

Example 4d

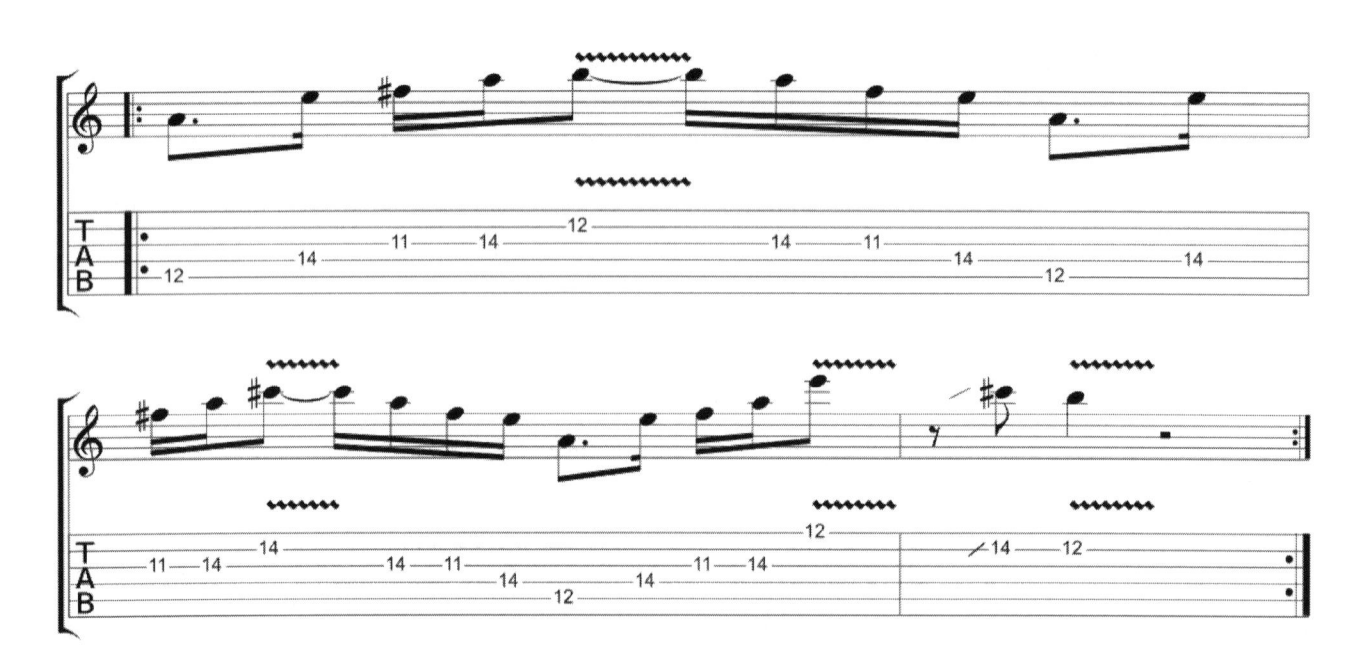

A Major Pentatonic – Position 5 'G' Shape

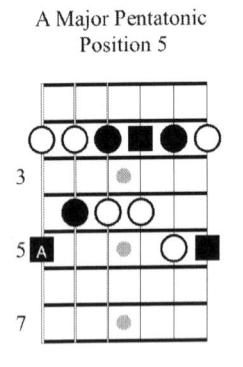

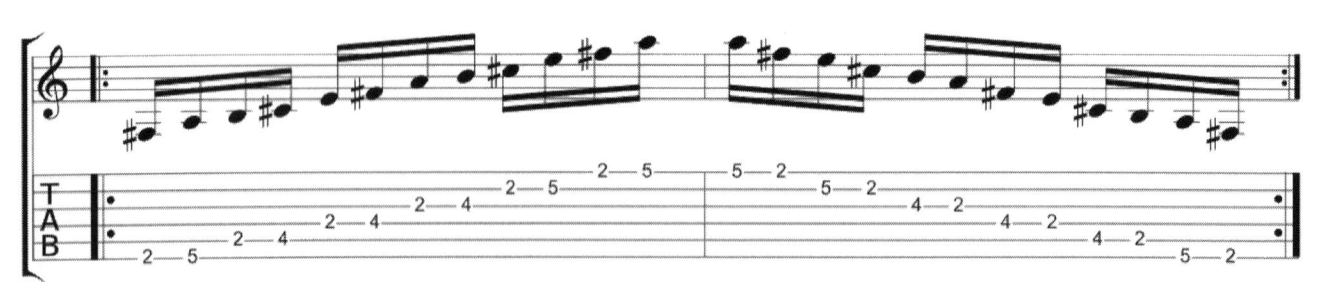

In example 4e we introduce a bending pattern that is popular in country music. It may feel uncomfortable to use your fourth finger to barre the top two strings at first, but developing the ability to barre your fourth finger is a useful skill.

Example 4e

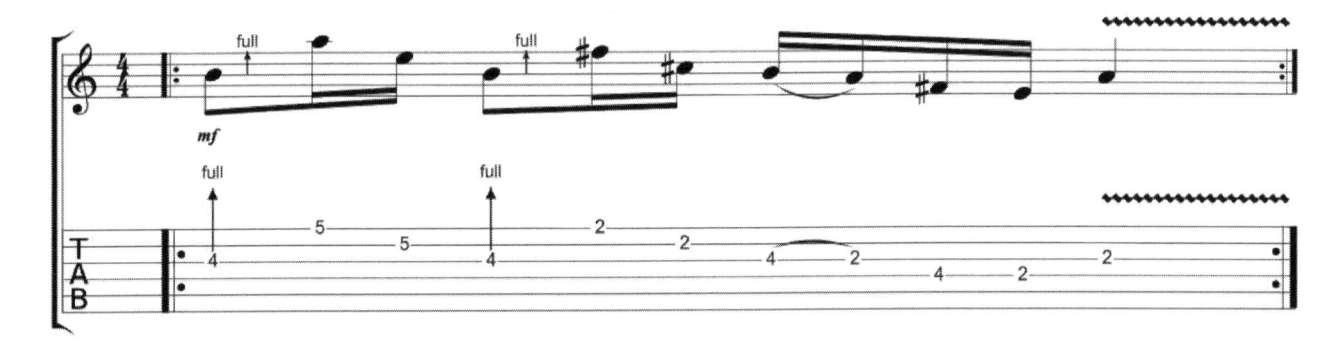

The licks shown in this chapter favour blues, country and rock, and Backing Track Two will compliment them perfectly. As with all the chapters in this book, practice the chord shape, the scale shape and then the lick. As soon as you are comfortable, play the lick over the backing track. The quicker you get used to playing these licks in context the better.

The Major Pentatonic scale will always have a happier sound than its minor counterpart, so bear that in mind when creating solos. It's important to base your scale choice on the mood of the piece you are writing.

As well as writing your own licks in each position and becoming proficient at improvising using the scales in this book, try to write licks that span the length of the fretboard. A simple way to do this is to pick two specific strings and analyse all the available notes from the scale.

Remember the square dots are the root notes and will be where your licks may want to resolve.

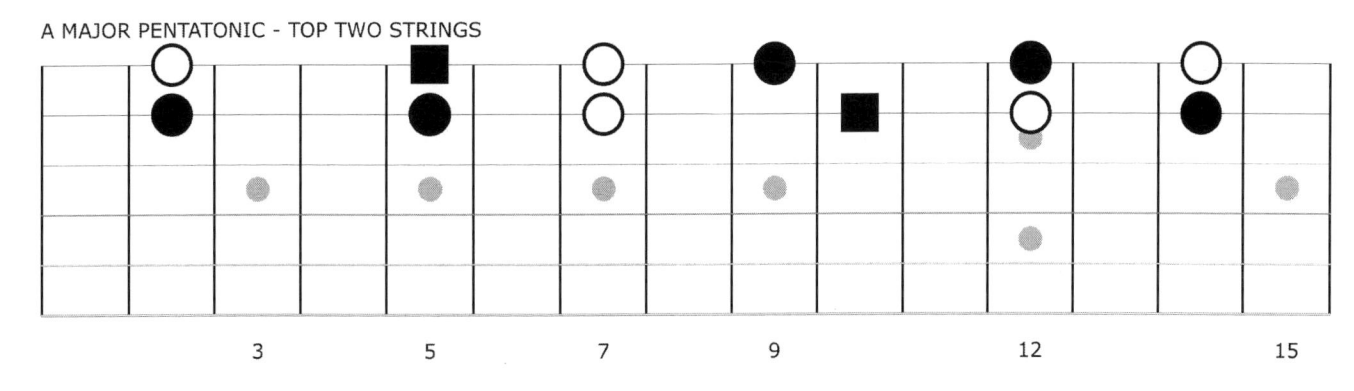

A MAJOR PENTATONIC - TOP TWO STRINGS

This diagram shows the notes of the A Major Pentatonic scale on the top two strings of the guitar. Using this diagram will help you to visualise the guitar in a linear fashion and helps you to break out of box position shapes.

On page 11 you can see the full Major Pentatonic scale shape on which this two-string approach is based.

27

Chapter Five: The 'Hindu' Pentatonic Scale

Video: www.fundamental-changes.com/exotic-pentatonic-soloing Password: hirojoshi

Backing Track Three

The 'Hindu' Pentatonic scale has a slightly Eastern flavour, and Eric Johnson and Jeff Beck are big fans of this sound.

In blues guitar, the Minor Pentatonic scale is often used over both minor and dominant 7th-type chords. The clash between the minor and major tonalities produces some of the soul of the blues. The 'Hindu' Pentatonic is another choice you can use when playing over dominant 7th chords.

The A 'Hindu' Pentatonic contains the notes of **A C# D E** and **G**. These are the notes of a dominant 7th chord (A C# E and G) with an added 4th (D). The only difference between the 'Hindu' Pentatonic and the Minor Pentatonic scale is that there is a major 3rd in the 'Hindu' Pentatonic scale compared to a minor 3rd in the Minor Pentatonic.

The formula for the 'Hindu' Pentatonic scale is 1 3 4 5 b7.

As there is only one note difference between the 'Hindu' Pentatonic and the Minor Pentatonic scale, it is easy to *adapt* a 'normal' Minor Pentatonic lick to create a new sound by changing just one note. For example, in the key of A, the note C in the Minor Pentatonic scale can be moved up by one semitone to C# to create the 'Hindu' Pentatonic scale.

The licks in this chapter work well over dominant 7 chords, and fit beautifully over a traditional 'dominant 7' 12-bar blues.

All of the following 'Hindu' Pentatonic scales are organised around dominant 7 CAGED chords. As always, make sure you learn the chord and scale shape first before attempting the licks.

A 'Hindu' Pentatonic – Position 1 'E' Shape

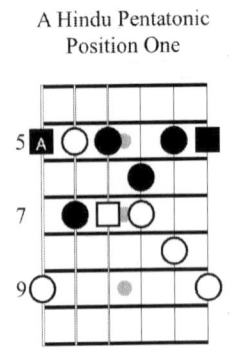

A Hindu Pentatonic
Position One

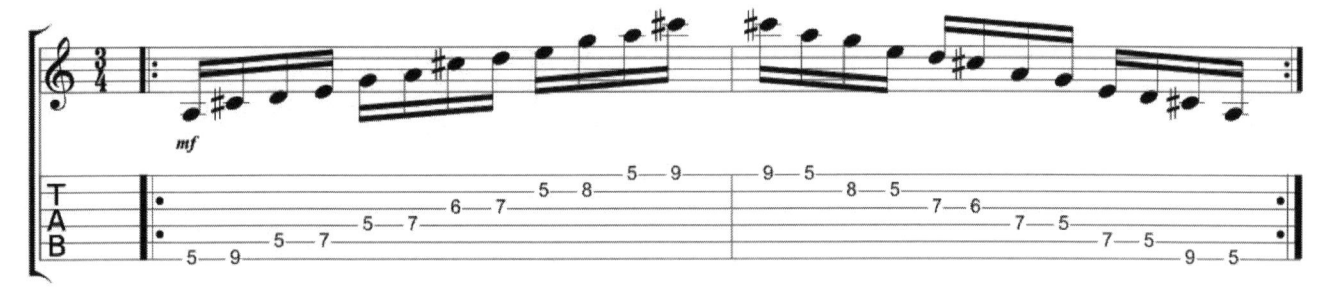

Example 5a uses a series of hammer-ons and pull-offs that are combined with bends and vibrato. In bar two, the stretch to the 9th fret may prove tricky at first, but training your fourth finger to stretch multiple frets comfortably is a vital skill. If you find this stretch tricky, try lowering the position of your wrist.

This lick is written over an A7 chord, but you should also learn it in the keys of 'D' and 'E' by moving the line up to the 10th or 12th fret. Over a blues in A, try playing the lick over each chord in turn so that by using just this one lick, you can navigate through the whole progression.

Example 5a:

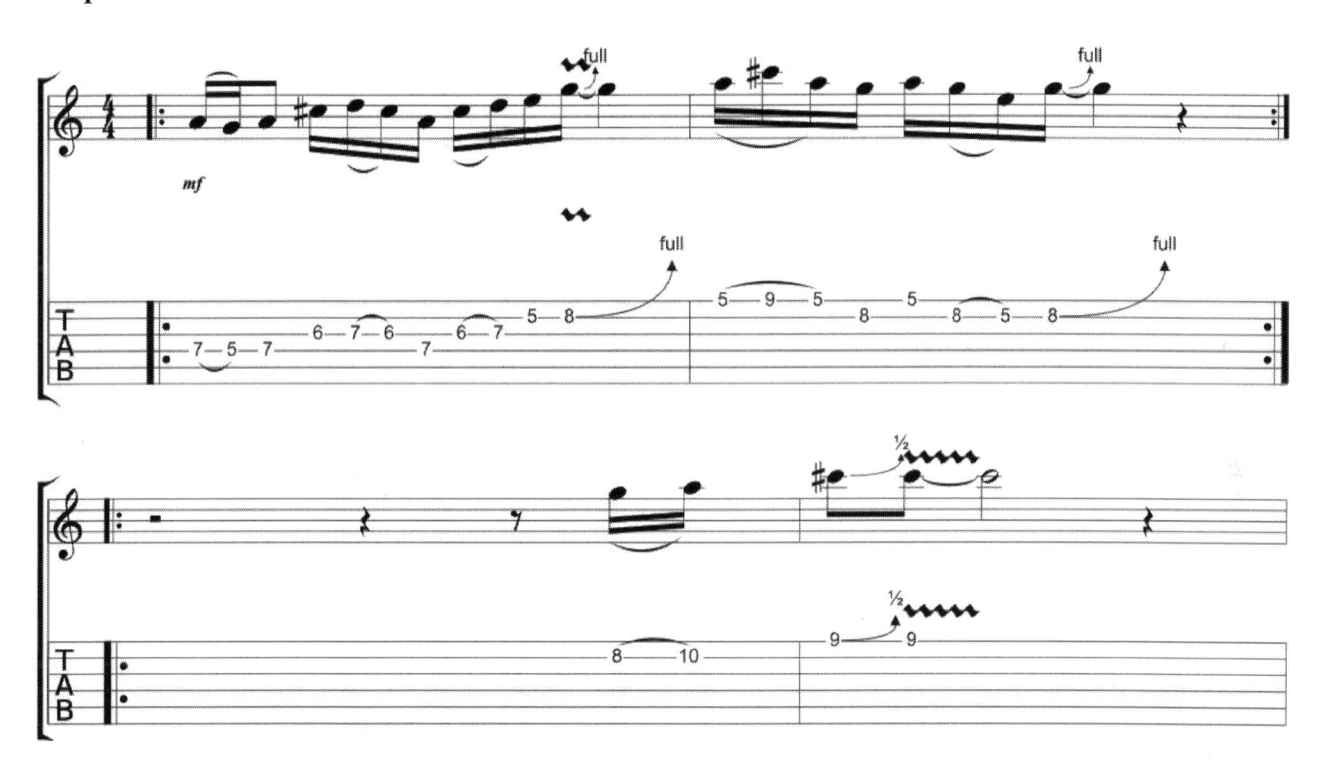

A 'Hindu' Pentatonic – Position 2 'D' Shape

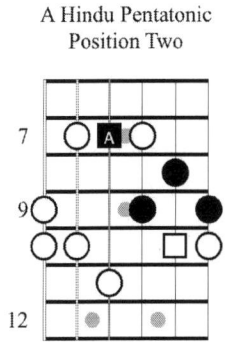

[Musical notation and tablature]

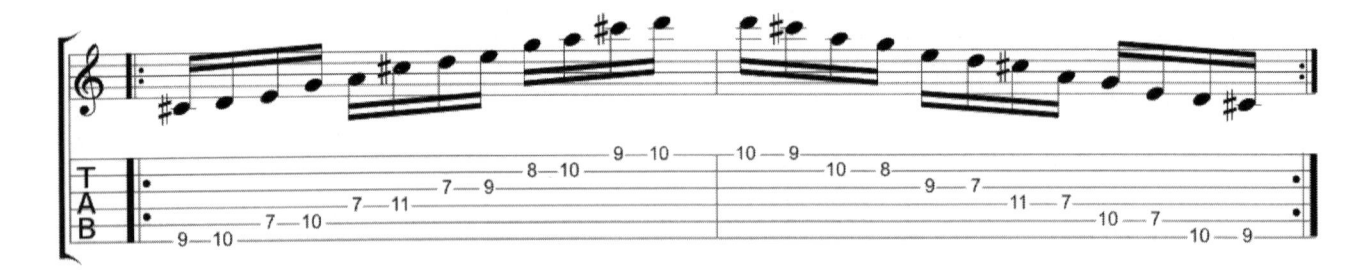

Example 5b is a blues lick with Eastern influences that written in the style of Jeff Beck. Although Jeff Beck is revered for his blues playing, he also blends fusion sounds into his songs. Listen to the Led Boots from the 1976 album Wired to hear some modern sounding 'Hindu' Pentatonic licks and phrasing.

Example 5b:

[Musical notation and tablature]

A 'Hindu' Pentatonic – Position 3 'C' Shape

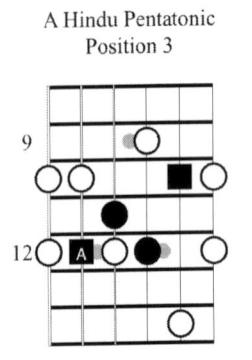

A Hindu Pentatonic
Position 3

[Fretboard diagram]

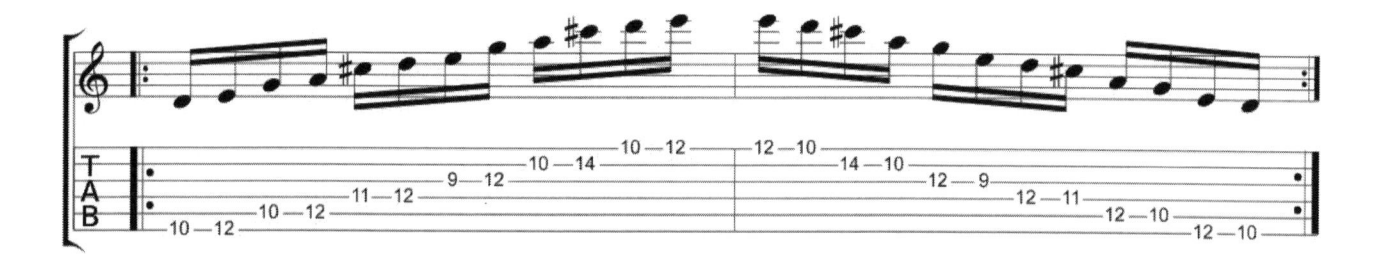

Example 5c introduces a unison bend. Jimi Hendrix and Carlos Santana both used unison bends in songs such as Crosstown Traffic and Samba Pa Ti.

Unison bends add a raw, vocal texture to your melodies.

Example 5c

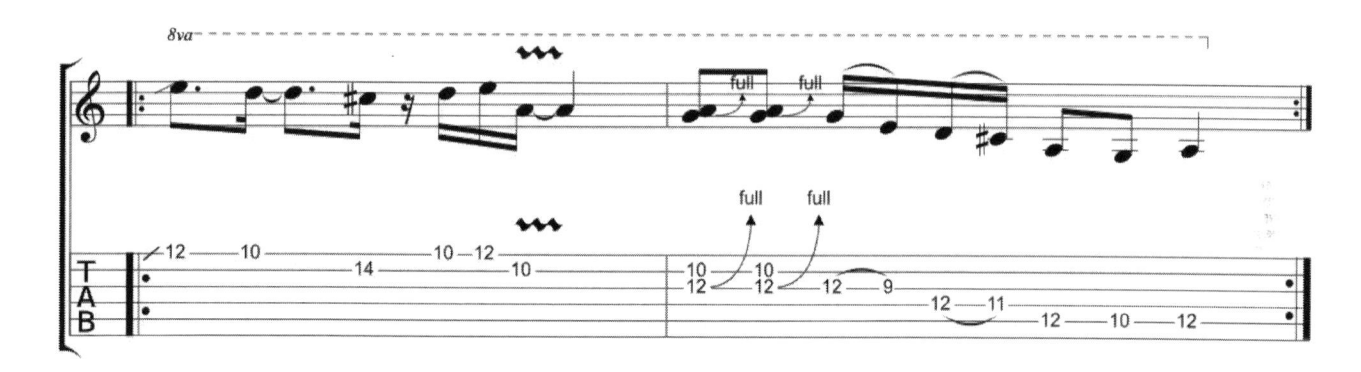

A 'Hindu' Pentatonic – Position 4 'A' Shape

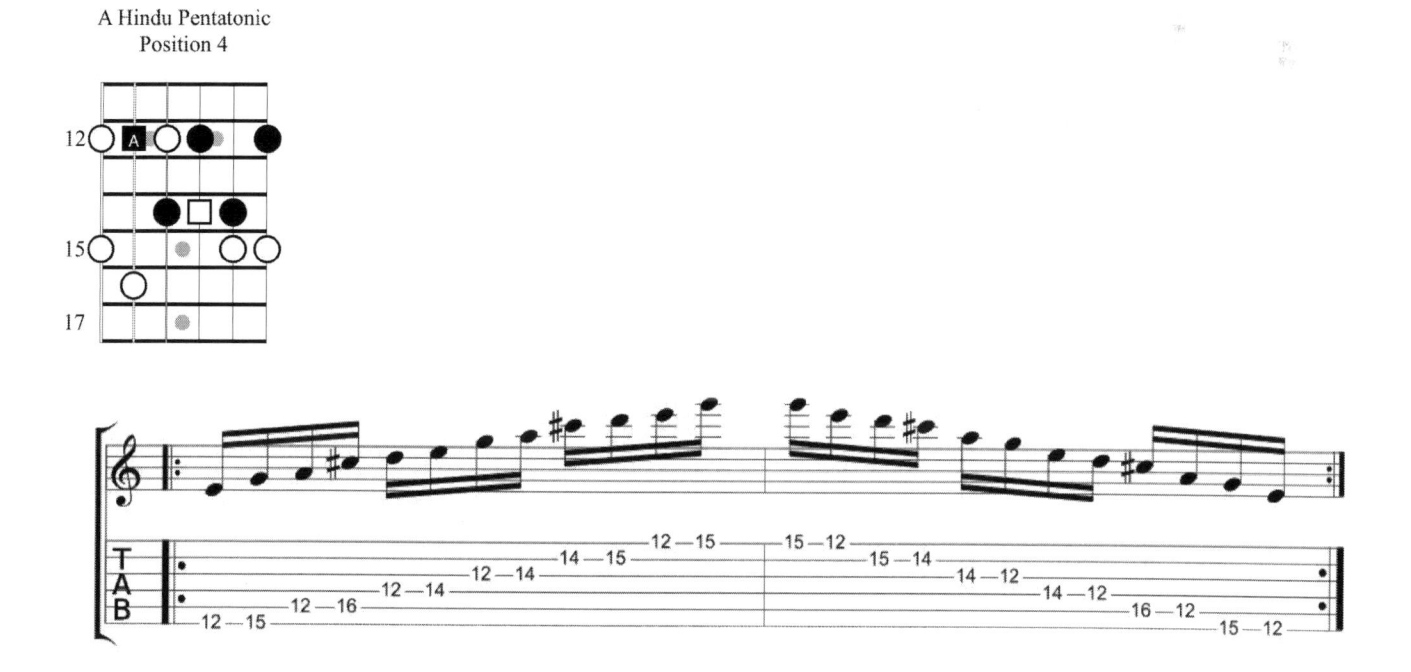

Each scale position creates different nuances in your playing, so certain bending or legato ideas may be better suited to some positions.

Example 5d is a fun line that is particularly suited to shape 4 of the 'Hindu' Pentatonic scale.

Example 5d

A 'Hindu' Pentatonic – Position 5 'G' Shape

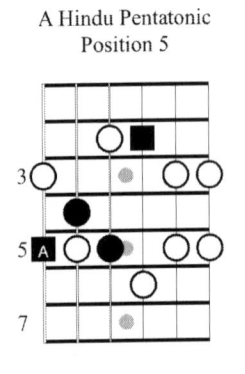

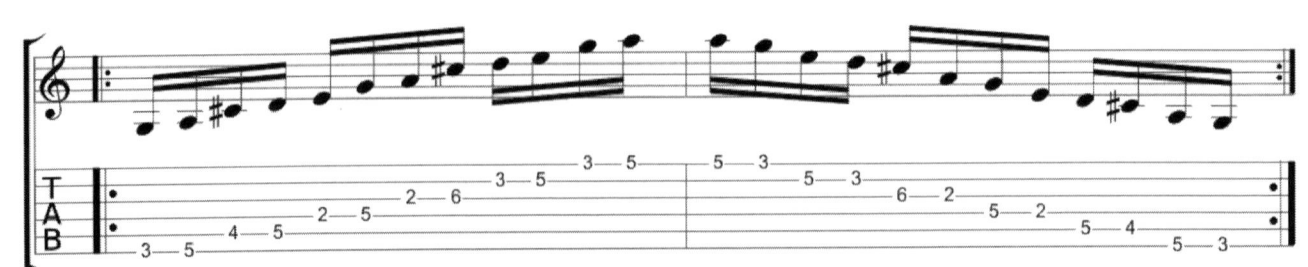

It can be fun to add dissonance to your melodies. Playing two notes that clash slightly is great in moderation!

Example 5e

Although the licks in this chapter are primarily rock and blues based, the 'Hindu' Pentatonic scale gives an Eastern twist to these examples. The 'Hindu' Pentatonic scale adds great contrast to the predominantly Minor Pentatonic melodies of Rock guitar.

In the Major Pentatonic chapter I showed you how to create a diagram that helps to span all five positions on the guitar using adjacent strings. This can also be done with *non-adjacent* strings.

Shown below is the A 'Hindu' Pentatonic scale on the B and the D strings. Try jumping between the strings to create wide intervallic leaps, or playing notes simultaneously to create large interval double stops.

Either finger pick these double stops or use a combination of your plectrum and your fingers (hybrid picking). You can use 'Backing Track Three' to practice these ideas.

A HINDU PENTATONIC - 2 STRINGS

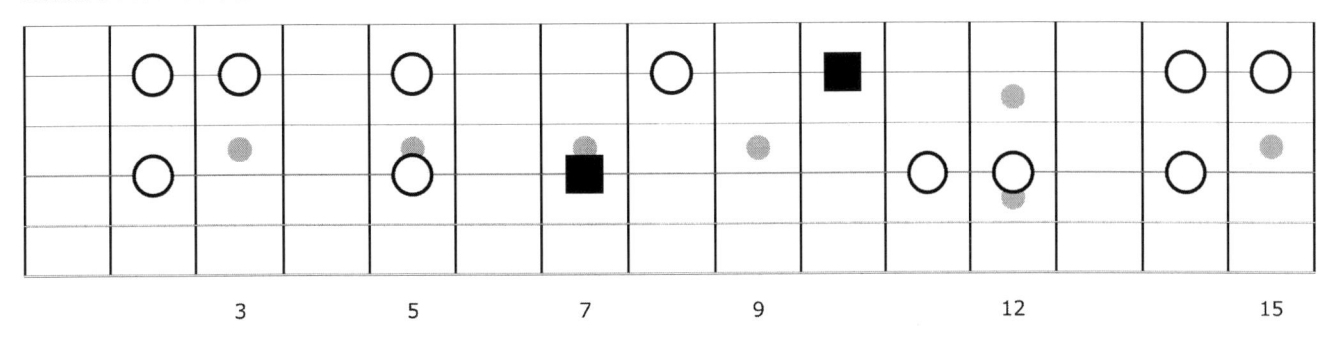

In the diagram below, all five CAGED A 'Hindu' Pentatonic scale shapes are laid out across the guitar. The square dots once again show you the 'A' root notes and acts as your anchor points for each shape.

By viewing all five CAGED shapes together in one diagram, you are less restricted to specific areas allowing you to create longer licks that cover more of the fretboard.

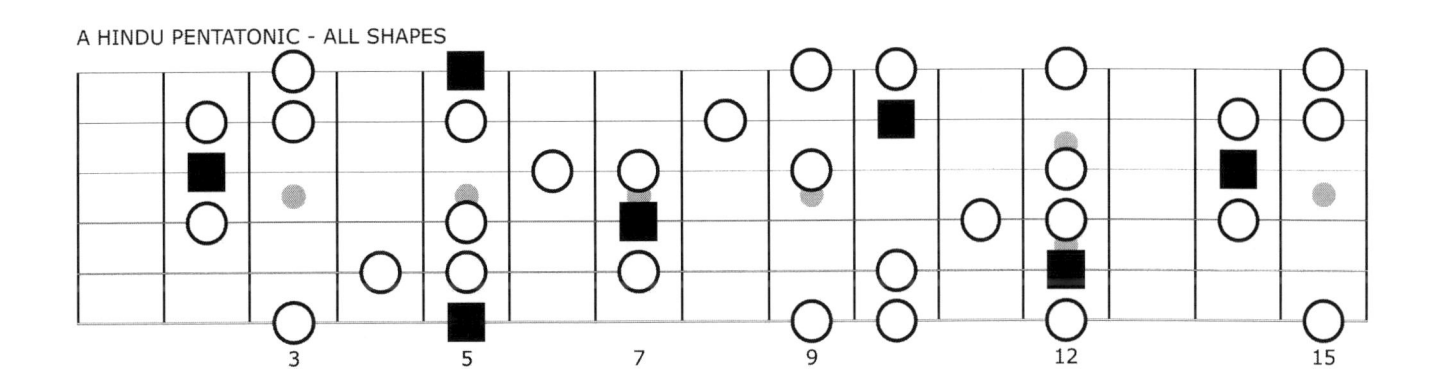

A HINDU PENTATONIC - ALL SHAPES

Chapter Six: The Blues Pentatonic Scale

Video: www.fundamental-changes.com/exotic-pentatonic-soloing Password: hirojoshi

Backing Track Six

The Blues Pentatonic scale has a modern sound but retains the flavour of its traditional heritage. This scale is most often used in blues, rock, metal and jazz.

The Blues Pentatonic scale derives from the commonly used six-note 'Blues' scale, but removes one interval (the 4th) to keep the pentatonic framework. Synyster Gates, guitarist in the hugely popular Avenged Sevenfold favours this scale.

The Blues Pentatonic scale contains the notes of **A C Eb E G** in the key of A. The 'character' note in this scale is the Eb, a dark diminished 5th interval giving the Blues Pentatonic a sinister sound that is popular with rock/metal guitarists.

The formula for the Blues Pentatonic scale is 1 b3 b5 5 b7.

The licks demonstrated here will work well over Am and A5 power chords and are more technically demanding, focussing on developing speed using hammer-ons, pull-offs and alternate picking. Try to follow the notated techniques closely and always learn each lick slowly before raising the tempo.

Try beginning with the metronome set at 70bpm, and when you can play your lick, riff, or chord progression perfectly three times in a row, move it up to 73bpm, then 76bpm, etc. By increasing the speed in steps of 3bpm you will work on all the interim speeds that are often neglected.

A Blues Pentatonic – Position 1 'E' Shape

The chords that fit the Blues Pentatonic scale are the Am CAGED shapes.

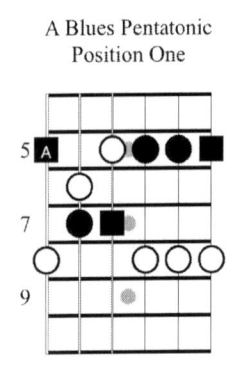

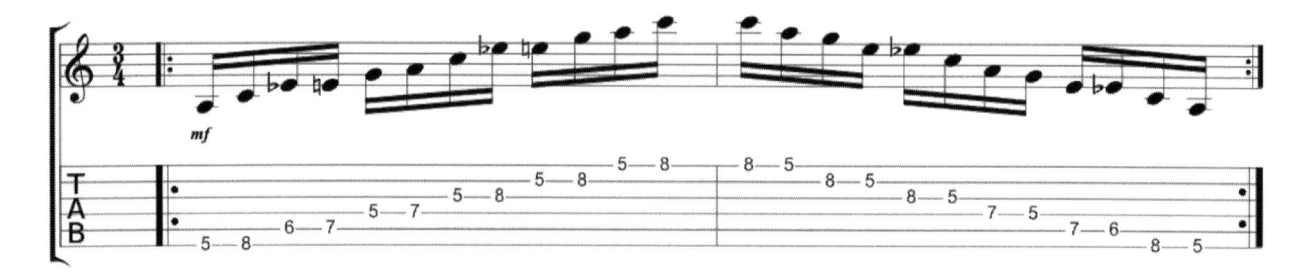

Example 6a demonstrates a classic, rock legato pattern. The sextuplets (groupings of six notes) are popular among modern players like Zakk Wylde. You can use either your ring finger or your little finger for the notes on the eighth fret.

When learning rock licks, make sure you always find a way to *exit* the lick. Playing a few repetitions of each pattern is usually enough before it becomes boring and monotonous. After you have found your 'exit point,' try finishing the lick with a bend or a slide.

Example 6a

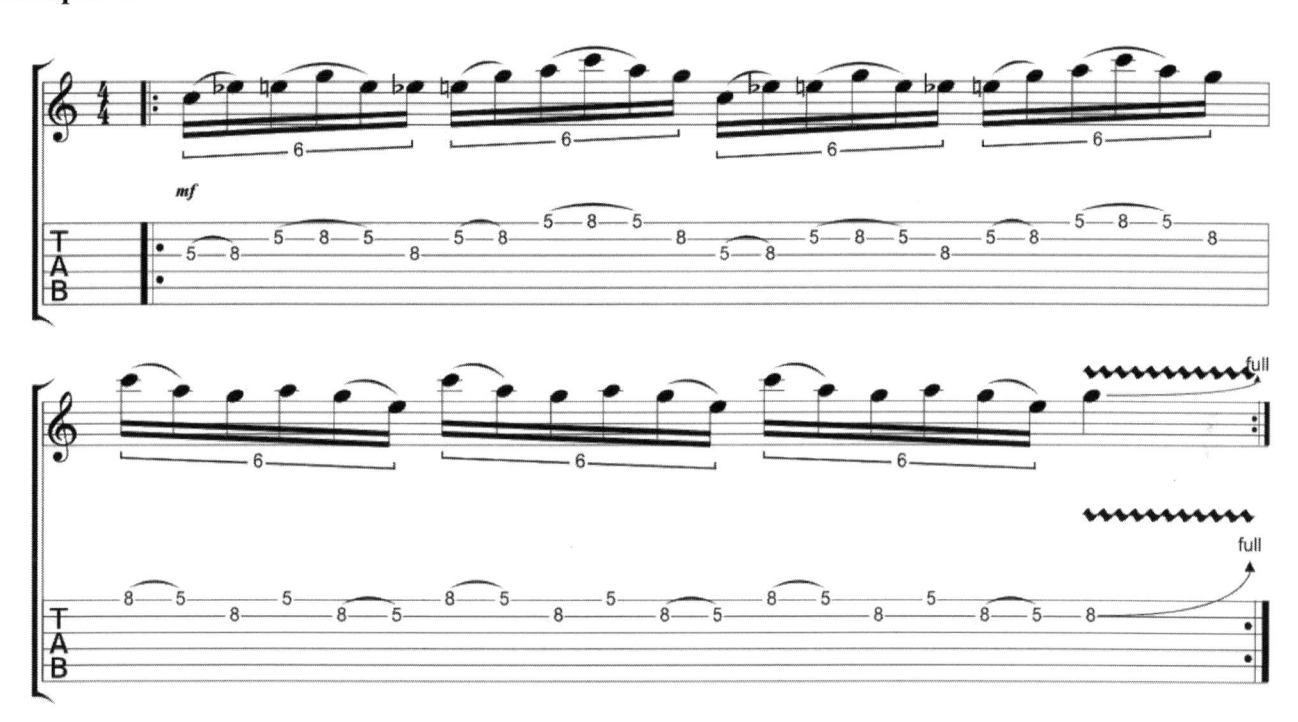

A Blues Pentatonic – Position 2 'D' Shape

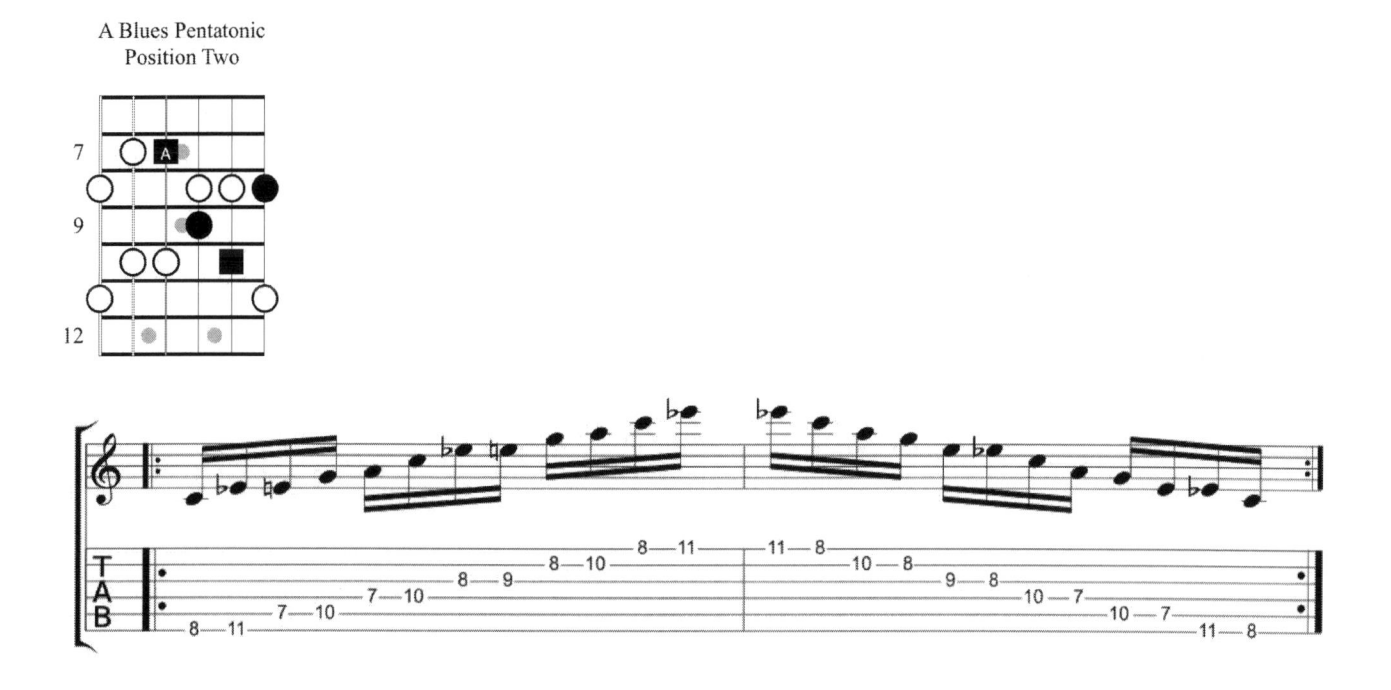

35

The following lick is reminiscent of the style of Synyster Gates. Experiment by adding palm muting to this lick by laying your picking hand gently across the guitar strings very close to the bridge. The ability to switch between palm muting and unmuted picking is useful for playing both rhythm playing and lead.

Vibrato is an important technique that is approached differently depending on the style of music. It is a hard technique to describe in words so watch the accompanying video to help you master the technique needed for rock vibrato.

Example 6b

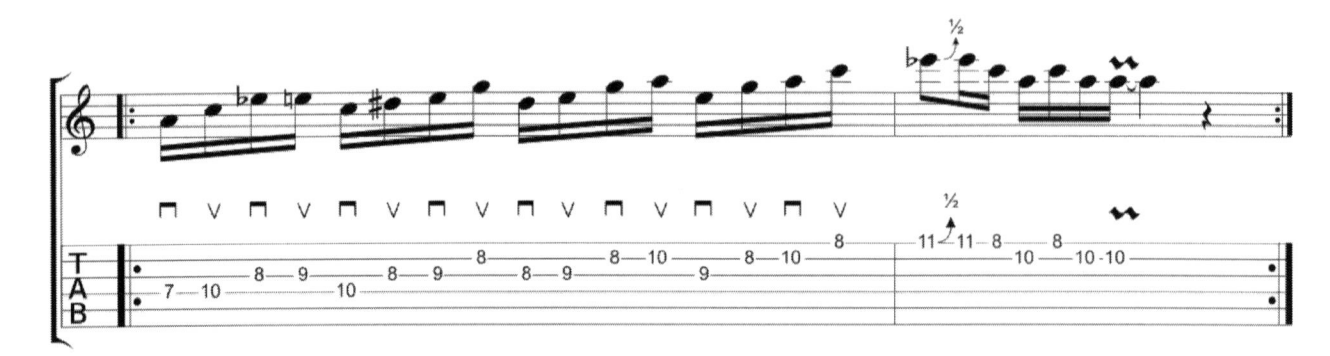

A Blues Pentatonic – Position 3 'C' Shape

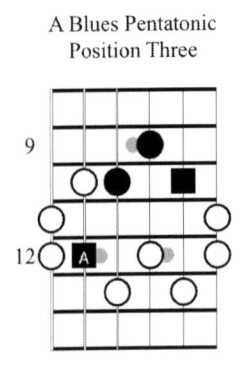

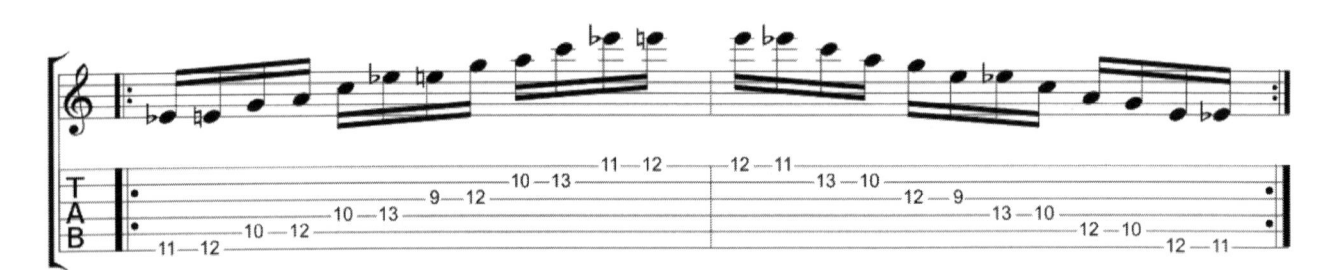

The next idea demonstrates a repeating pattern commonly seen in rock that uses hammer-ons and pull-offs. By incorporating speedier legato phrases into your playing you can blend soft emotive blues licks with rapid-fire rock lines to create speed variations in your solos.

Example 6c

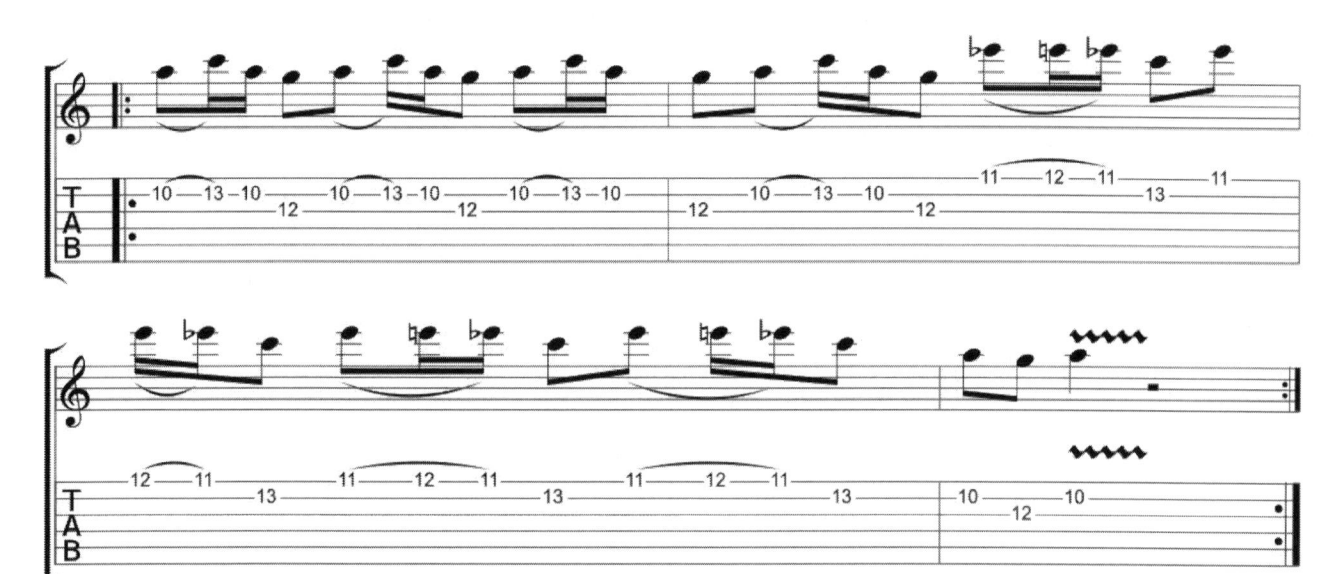

A Blues Pentatonic – Position 4 'A' Shape

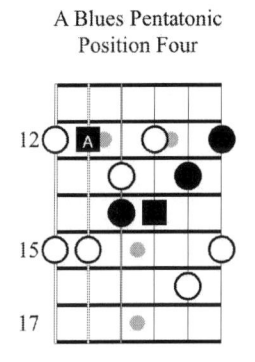

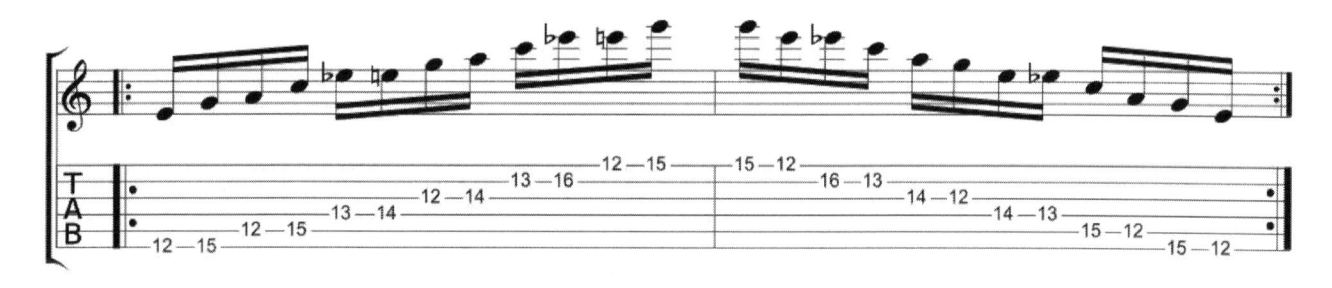

A Blues Pentatonic
Position Four

37

Example 6d

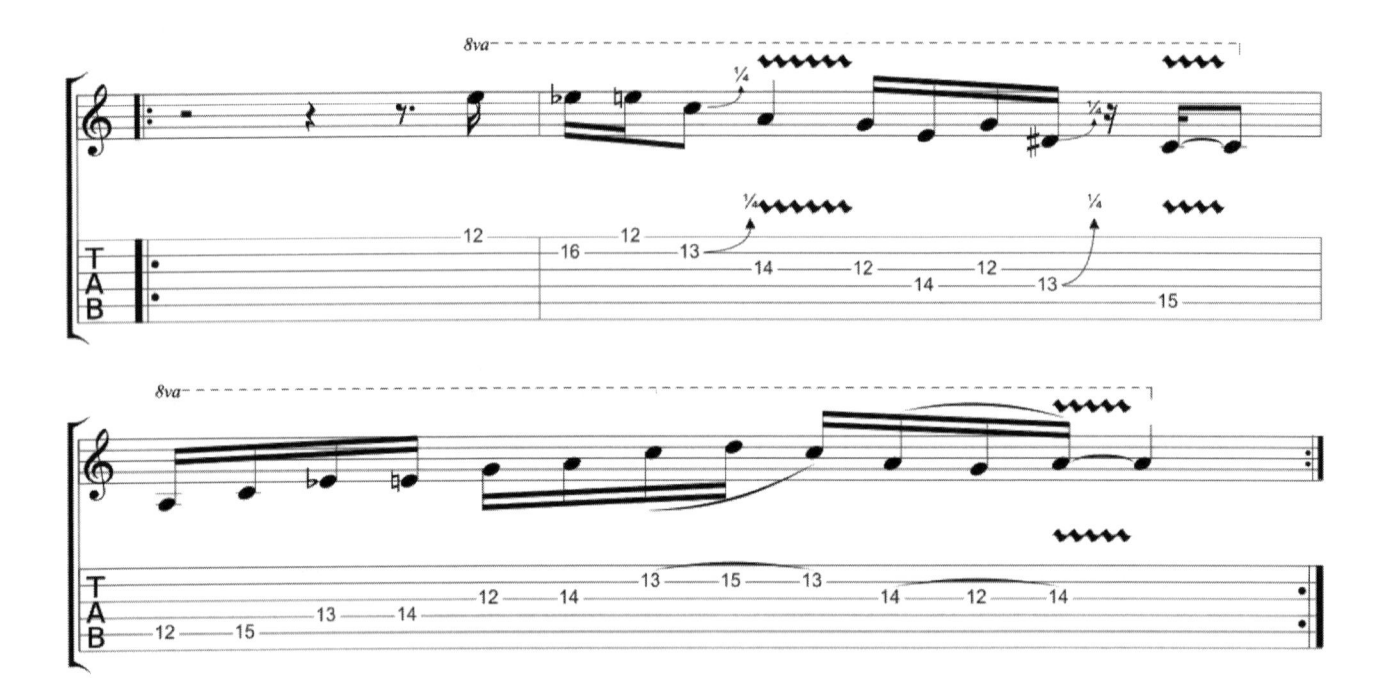

Example 6d uses 'bluesy' quarter-tone bends known as *curls*. A blues curl is normally the smallest audible distance you can bend a string on the guitar. Watch the video to see how I play blues curl bends within this lick.

John Mayer's version of the blues anthem Crossroads on the album Battle Studies is a bending masterclass. He uses the blues curl to great effect in the solo and demonstrates the nuance of string bending.

A Blues Pentatonic – Position 5 'G' Shape

38

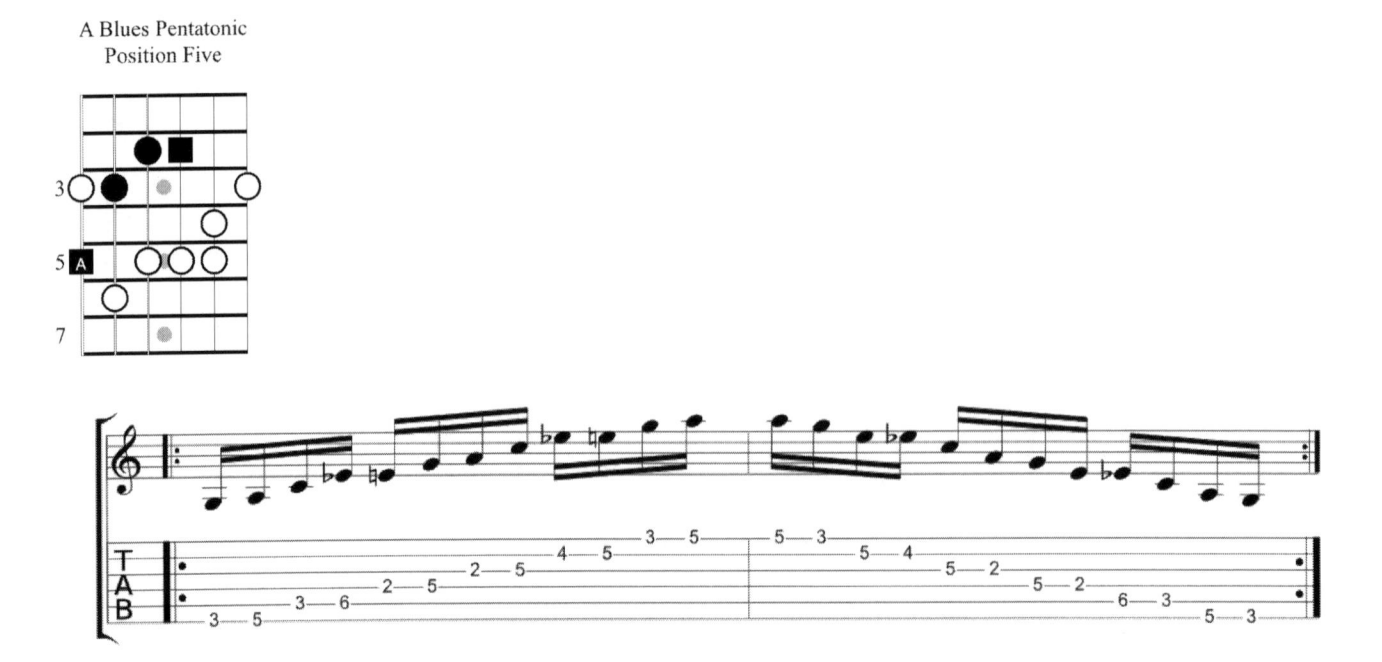

Example 6e shows another way of creating speed-based rock patterns by using legato to create mini trills.

Trills are a great rock technique that sound difficult but with practice become very easy. Ritchie Blackmore uses this idea to great effect.

Example 6e

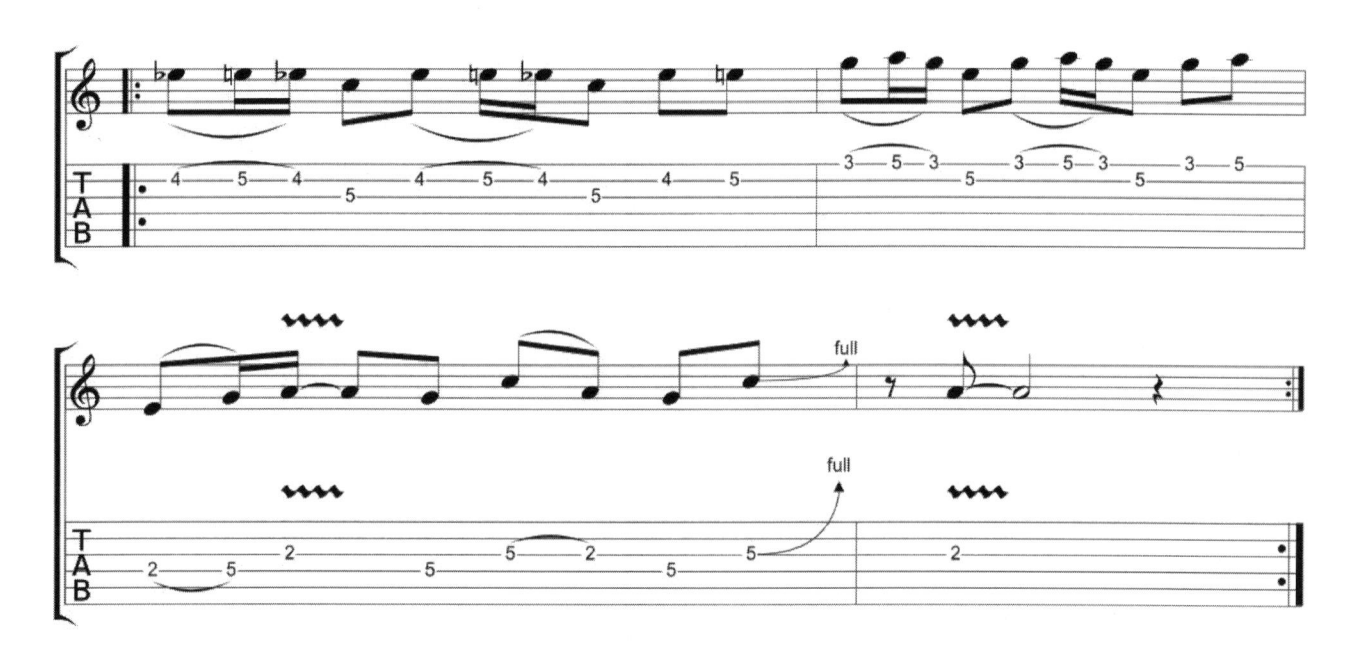

Enhancing your technique should become part of your core practice regime. Set yourself clear goals in your technique practice, for example, you could aim to play example 6b at 80bpm in thirty days time.

Begin very slowly with a metronome set at 50bpm and make sure every note is clean and audible. Watch your picking hand and notice if you are applying the strict 'down, up' alternate picking pattern required.

When you can play example 6b perfectly three times in a row at 50bpm, try raising the metronome up to 53bpm. Continue to increase the metronome speed in increments of 3 beats-per-minute up to your goal speed of 80bpm.

This form of structured practice means that you will only increase your speed once the lick is played accurately. Make sure you listen to the slowed-down audio examples of each lick as well as the full speed versions, to help you develop accuracy at slower speeds.

Chapter Seven: The Robben Ford Pentatonic Scale

Video: www.fundamental-changes.com/exotic-pentatonic-soloing Password: hirojoshi

Backing Track Six

Robben Ford is a jazz-blues superstar. Ford's use of sophisticated jazz lines and soulful, earthy blues licks combine to make him a hero to many guitarists. The Robben Ford Pentatonic scale has a jazzy sound and will make your playing sound more hip. The Robben Ford Pentatonic scale is more correctly named the *Minor 6th Pentatonic scale* or the *Dorian Pentatonic scale*, and replaces the b7 in the Minor Pentatonic scale with the natural 6th note from the Dorian mode.

The Robben Ford Pentatonic scale contains the notes **A C D E F#** in the key of A. The addition of the F# gives the scale its character.

The formula for the Robben Ford Pentatonic scale is 1 b3 4 5 6.

The licks presented in this chapter fit perfectly over an Am6 chord. Shown below is a popular, jazzy Am6 chord voicing.

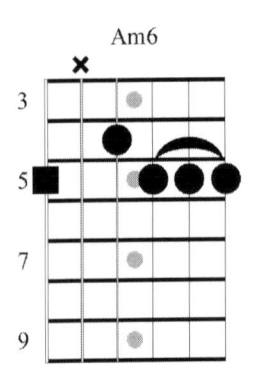

As the Robben Ford Pentatonic is a minor based scale so once again the Am CAGED shapes accompany the following scales.

A Robben Ford Pentatonic – Position 1 'E' Shape

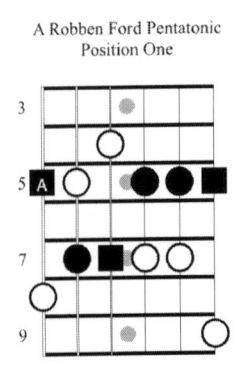

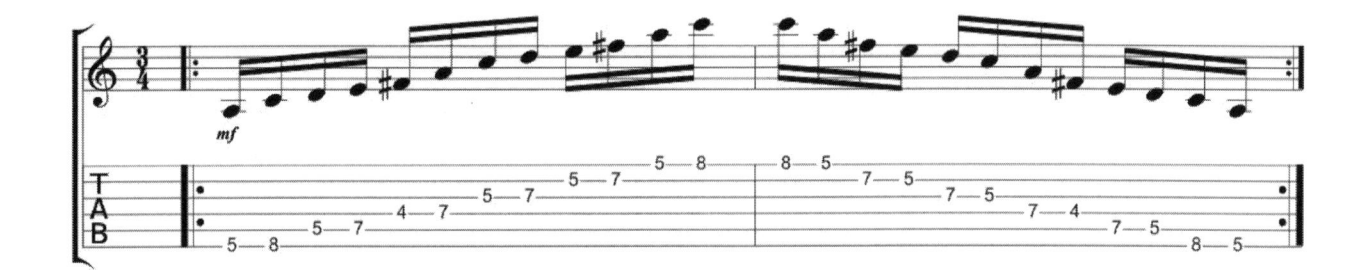

Example 7a shows how similar the Robben Ford Pentatonic is to the Minor Pentatonic scale. I love the classic bluesy sound of this lick combined with the exciting new flavours of the additional 6th (F#). Bar two is a lick in itself, which introduces a double stop phrase that is memorable and fun to play.

Example 7a

A Robben Ford Pentatonic – Position 2 'D' Shape

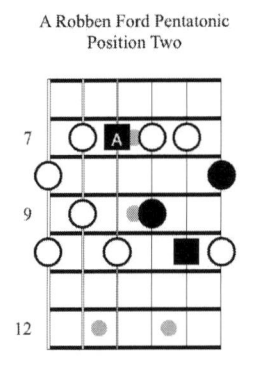

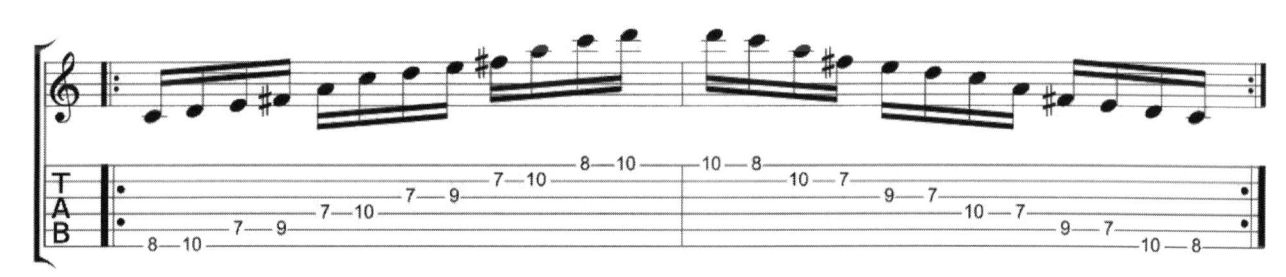

Mozart famously said, "The music is not in the notes, but the silence in between". As guitarists, we often overplay; favouring endless note runs over simpler phrases with audible pauses. Example 7b demonstrates how to use rests between passages of notes to create space to highlight each lick.

Example 7b

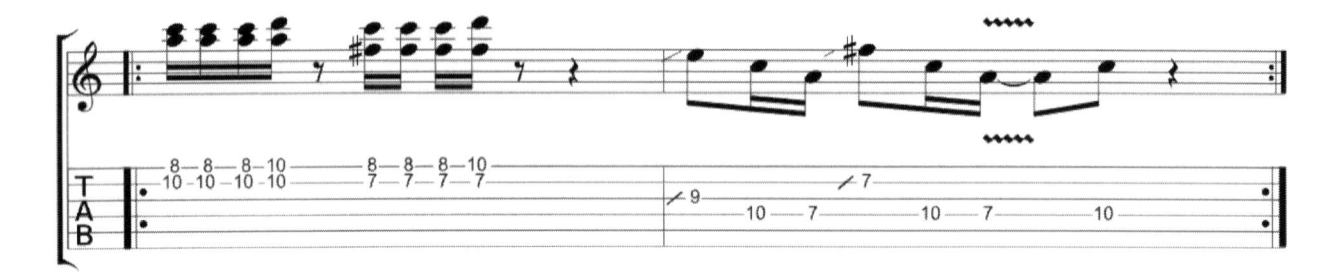

A Robben Ford Pentatonic – Position 3 'C' Shape

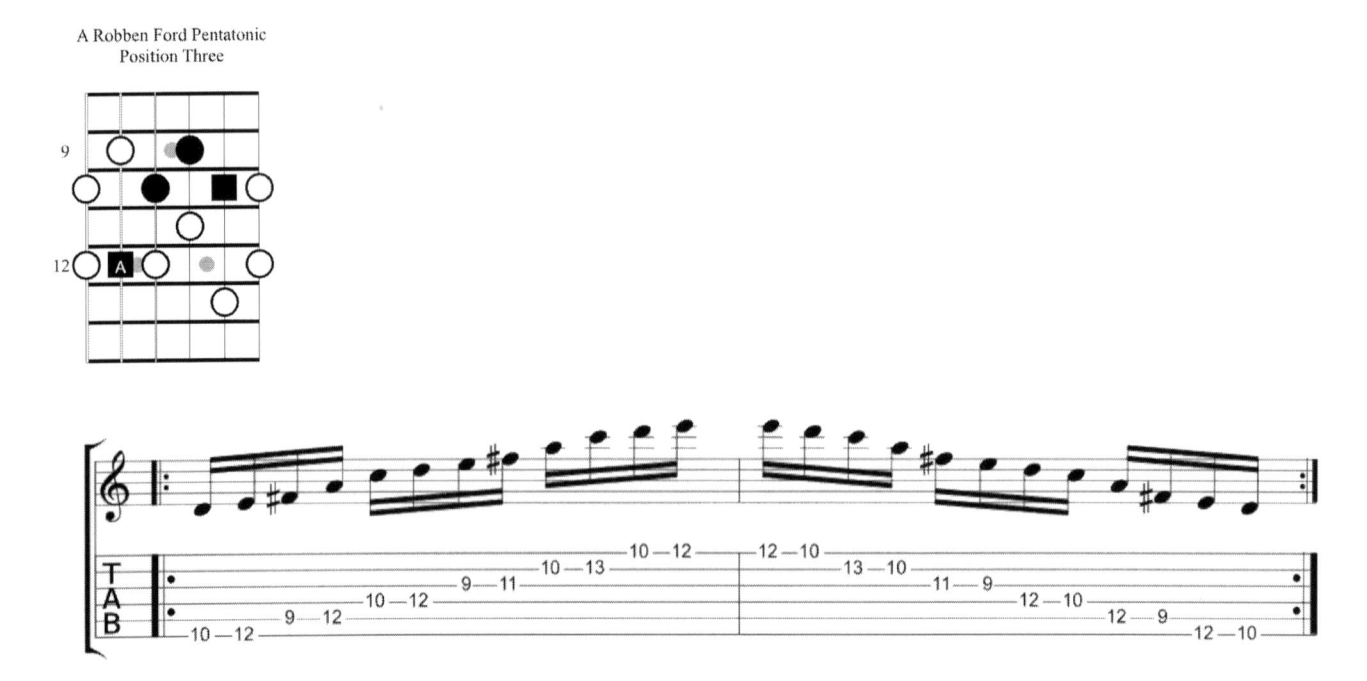

Example 7c is a *call and response*, double-stop pattern using some funky mutes. This idea could act as the central theme to a solo.

Example 7c

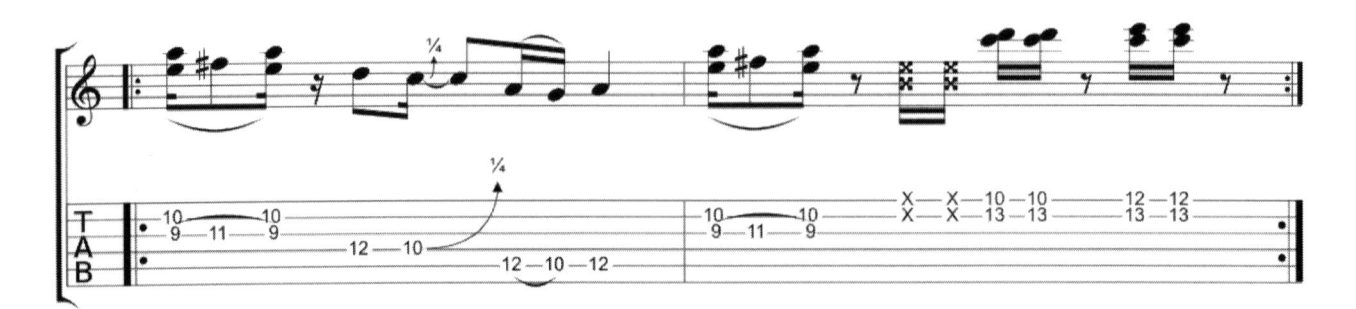

A Robben Ford Pentatonic – Position 4 'A' Shape

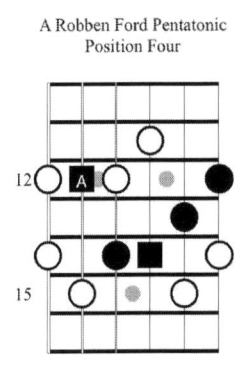

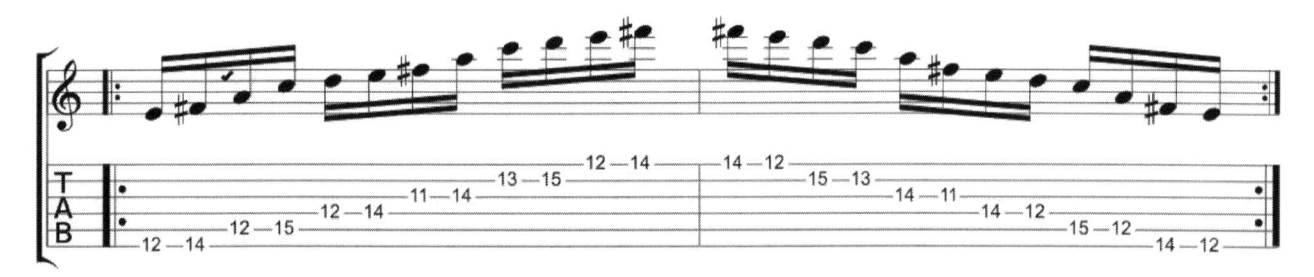

In this example, there are some half- and quarter-tone bends. Robben Ford's background in blues helps him to add gorgeous bends to his jazz-based phrasing.

I have added extra emphasis to the major 6th (F#) in this example by making it the centre of the lick. When you are writing new licks and ideas using the scales in this book aim to highlight the unique notes of each scale.

Example 7d

A Robben Ford Pentatonic – Position 5 'G' Shape

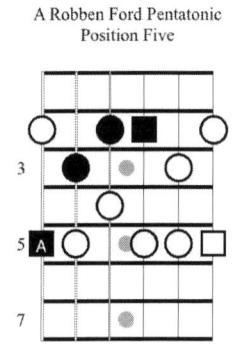

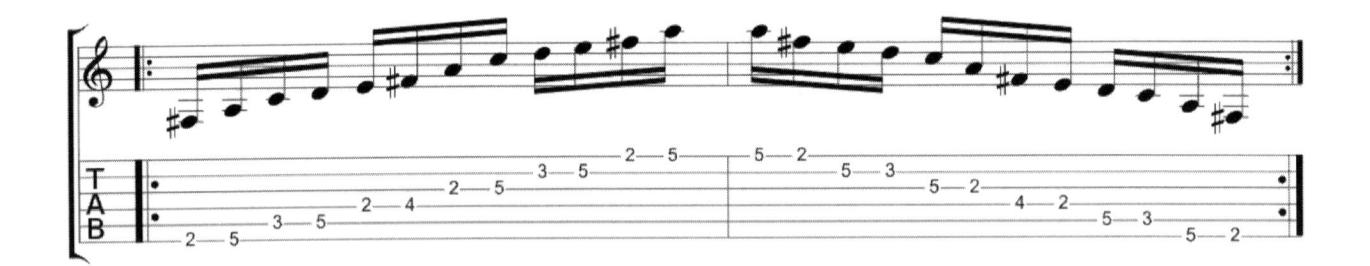

This example has a moody, funky blues feel. Try playing this lick twelve frets above where it is notated as well as in the position shown. By learning this lick in two different places you can connect it more easily with the other licks you have been learning.

As always, make sure you play licks different keys; don't get stuck playing everything in the key of A.

Example 7e

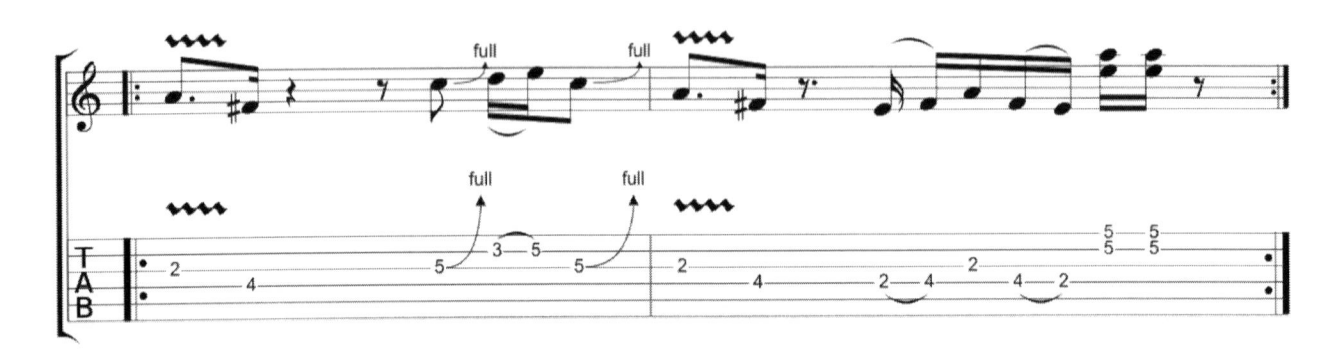

Play the licks in this chapter along with Backing Track Six and be sure to practice 'the art of silence' when creating your own improvisations, as this simple addition that will make your solos sound constructed and well-phrased.

Try combining the technical lines shown in the Blues Pentatonic chapter with the more delicately crafted rhythmic phrases shown here to create a wide variety of solos in different styles of music.

By this point in the book you should be realising that by changing just one note in a Minor Pentatonic scale you can create completely different and beautiful sounds.

Chapter Eight: The 'No Root add9' Pentatonic Scale

Video: www.fundamental-changes.com/exotic-pentatonic-soloing Password: hirojoshi

Backing Track One

This pentatonic scale has a fancy name but this really just means that the root note (A) has been removed and replaced by the 2nd/9th interval (B).

Guitarists who favour this sound include Eric Johnson and Joe Bonamassa. Both Johnson and Bonamassa are forward-thinking blues/rock guitarists, and this modern sounding scale is a perfect fit in their solos.

The 'No Root add9' Pentatonic scale contains the notes of **B C D E G** in the key of A.

The formula for the 'No Root add9' pentatonic scale is 2 b3 4 5 b7.

The addition of the 2nd/9th gives this scale a unique sound. Often as guitarists, we fall into the trap of always resolving back to a root note. This scale will help break that habit.

The licks in this chapter will fit perfectly over an Am9 chord. They will also work well with Backing Track One.

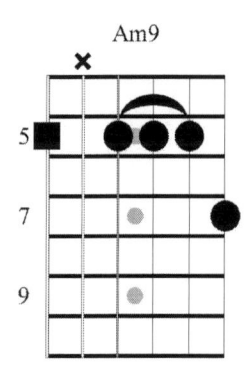

As the 'No Root add 9' Minor Pentatonic scale doesn't contain a root note, included in the diagrams are 'phantom' root notes shown using a grey diamond. *This note is for reference only and should not be played as part of the scale shape.*

A 'No Root add9' Pentatonic – Position 1 'E' Shape

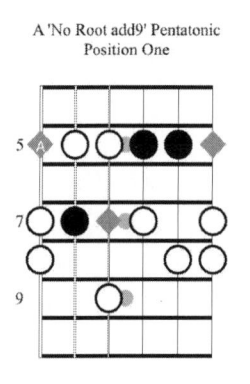

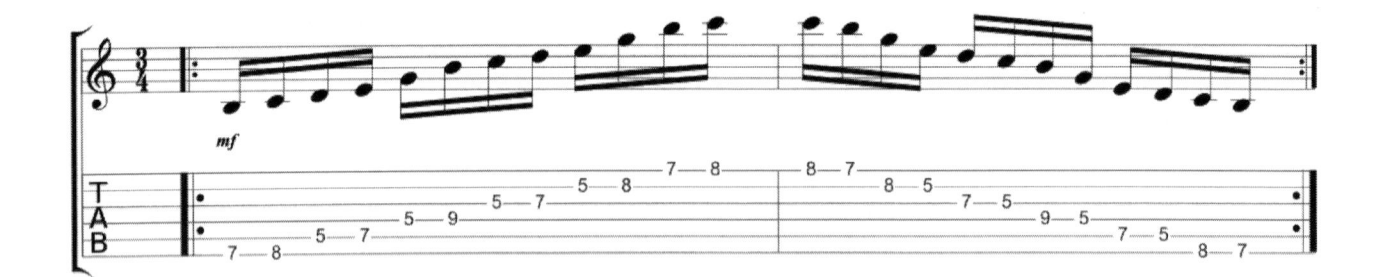

Sliding up or down on one string before skipping a string and doing the reverse (as shown in bars three and four), is an exciting way to approach scale shapes. Remember that slides can act as both a melodic tool and a bridge between scale shapes on the guitar. Guthrie Govan uses this idea to great effect on his track Waves.

Example 8a

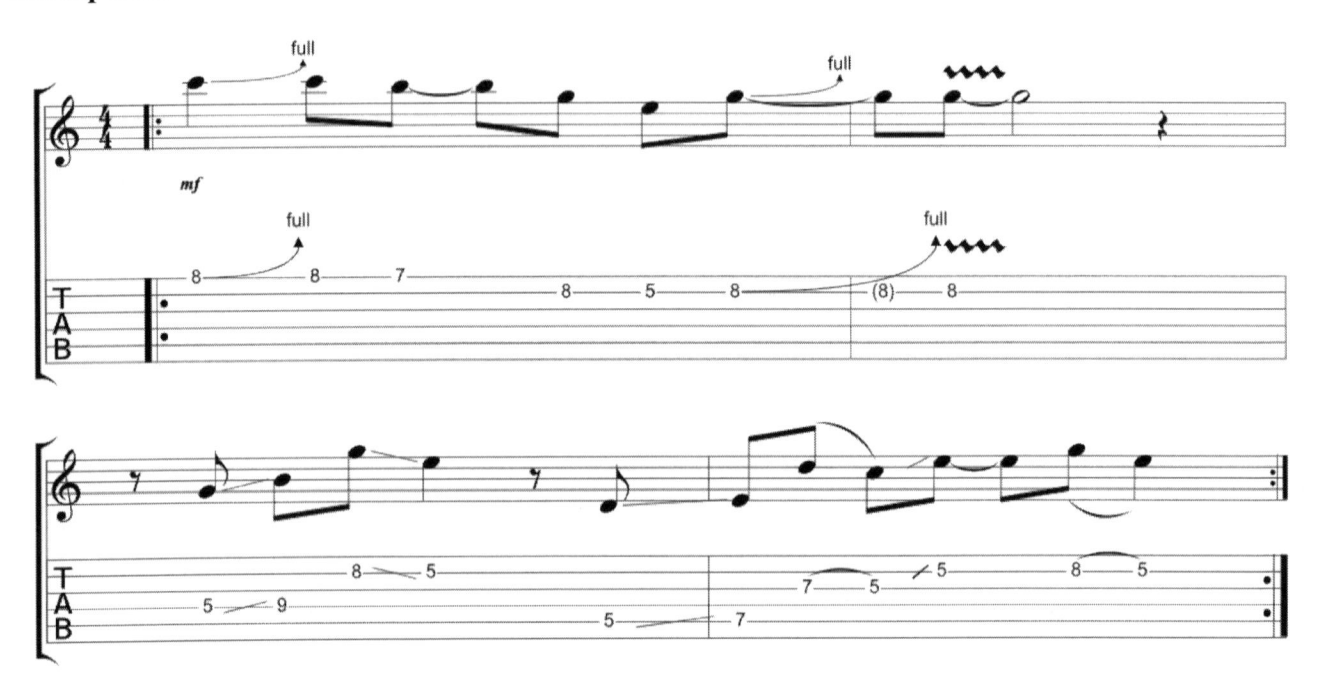

A 'No Root add9' Pentatonic – Position 2 'D' Shape

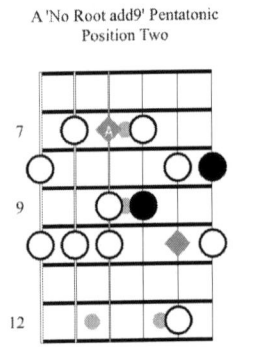

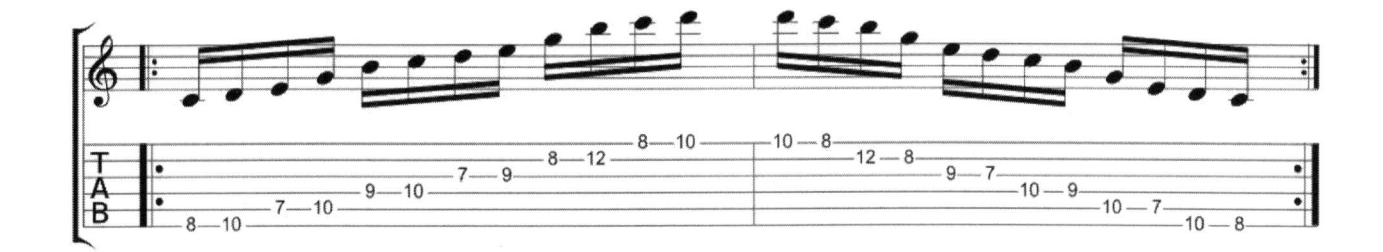

Although simple, this next lick has a vocal quality to it. Bar four shows you that you can get great value for money from just two notes.

Example 8b

A 'No Root add9' Pentatonic – Position 3 'C' Shape

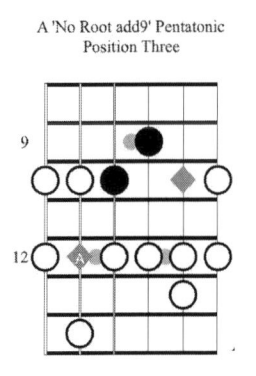

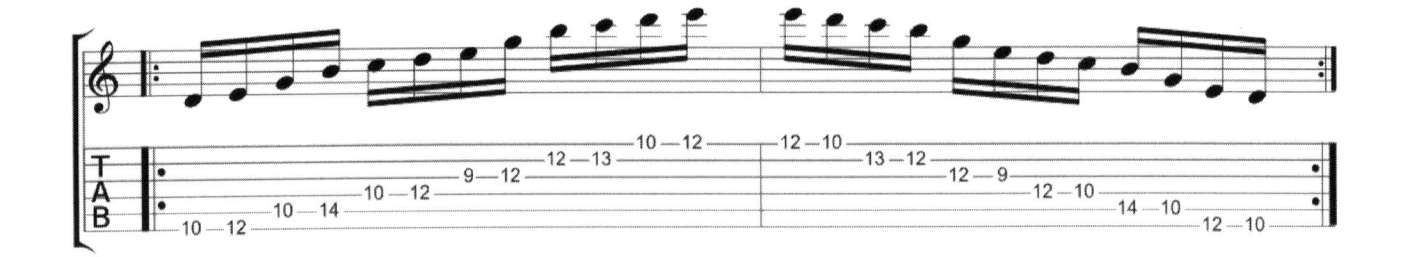

David Gilmour's effortless touch and control are wonderful to mimic and emulate. Bars one and two in the next example include a simple bend and vibrato pattern.

If you are struggling to get your bends in tune, play the note you are targeting first and then aim for that pitch when bending from the lower note. For example, in bar one we are bending the twelfth fret of the B string up by one fret. By playing the thirteenth fret (C) on the B string first, you will have a target to aim for with your bend.

Example 8c

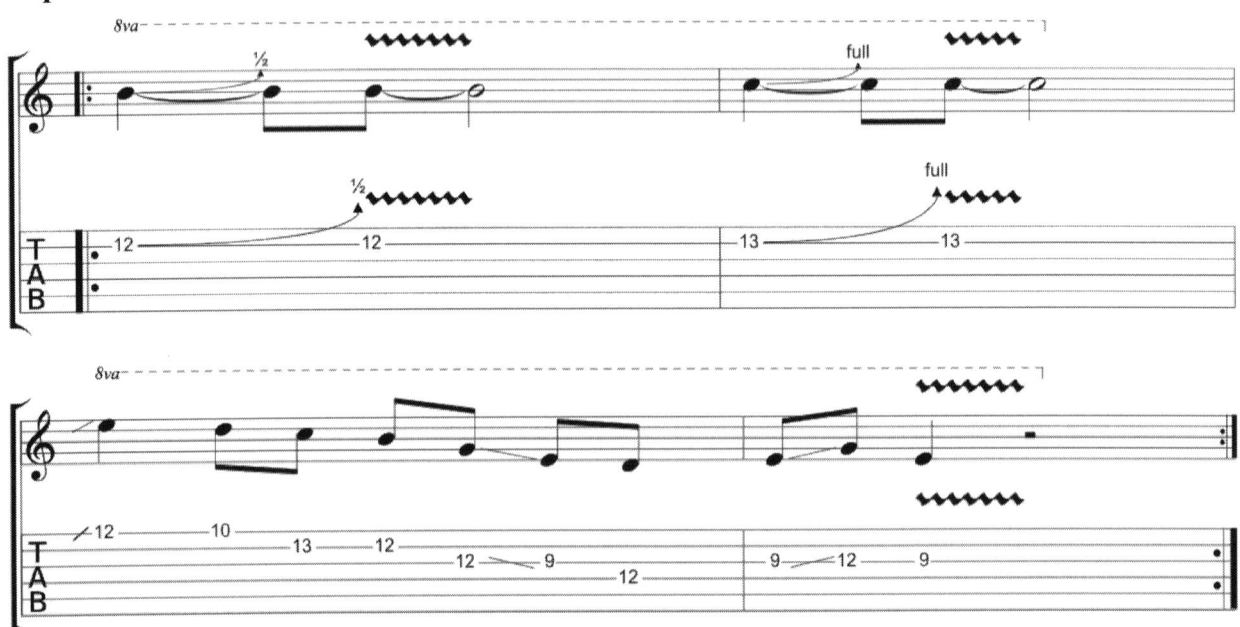

A 'No Root add9' Pentatonic – Position 4 'A' Shape

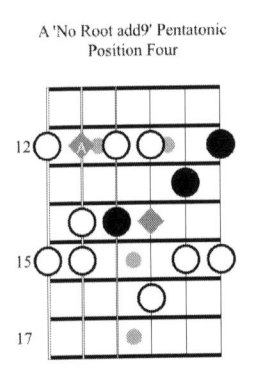

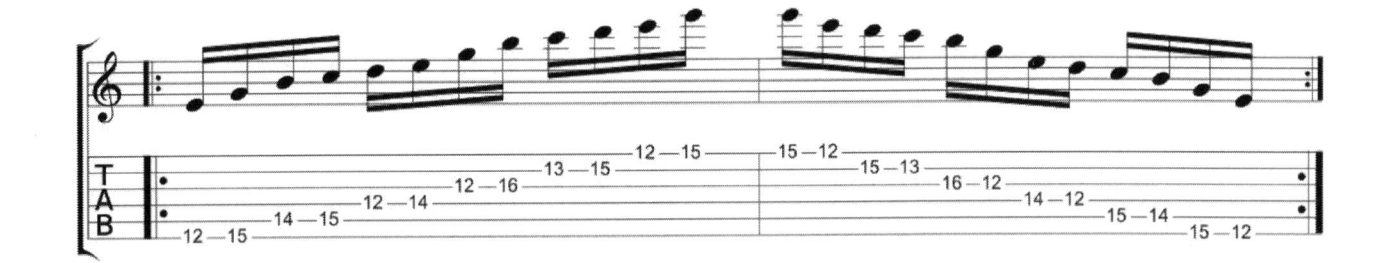

Example 8d is jumpy and edgy. The mixture of the upbeat rhythmic pattern and rests holds the listener's attention. On the bend in bar two, ensure you have your little finger on the top string as soon as you bend on the 'B' string. That way the notes can ring out into each other, a hugely popular sound in classic rock guitar.

Watch the video attached to this lick to see how I ring these notes together.

Example 8d

A 'No Root Add9 Pentatonic' – Position 5 'G' Shape

Example 8e utilises classic rock hammer-ons, vibrato and double stops. This lick is reminiscent of the solo in the track All Right Now, by Free, with the formidable Paul Rodgers on guitar.

Try playing this lick in the position shown below, and then move it up by twelve frets (an octave). The trick of moving the same lick twelve frets apart is very common in rock guitar solos.

Example 8e

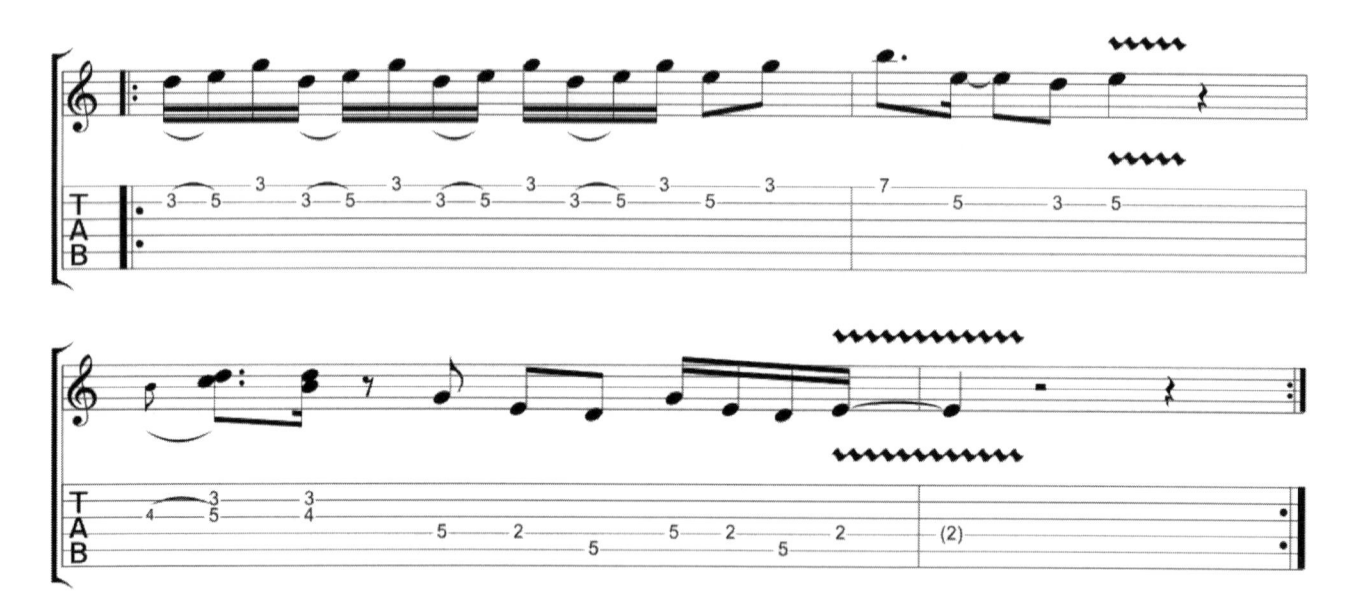

This chapter's licks favour rock and blues, so Backing Track One is the perfect option for practicing these examples. The 'no root add 9' pentatonic licks can feel slightly unresolved when playing over this backing track, as they never resolve to the home note of A. Embrace it!

Often guitarists end licks by targeting the root note of the scale. Aim to break out of this habit by deliberately ending on a different note of the pentatonic scale.

Where you start and end a lick are both important so always pay close attention to your note choice when creating solos.

Chapter Nine: The Lydian Pentatonic Scale

Video: www.fundamental-changes.com/exotic-pentatonic-soloing Password: hirojoshi

Backing Track Four

In the Lydian Pentatonic scale we isolate the qualities that define the Lydian mode (the 3rd, #4th and 7th intervals), and create a five note pentatonic pattern that is easy to use and apply. The Lydian pentatonic sound gives a unique vibe, perfect for modern rock and jazz.

Both Joe Satriani and Steve Vai favour the Lydian mode and they are two of the most groundbreaking rock guitarists of the post-Hendrix era. They are always searching for different, creative sounds for their instrumental albums.

The Lydian Pentatonic scale contains the notes **A C# D# E G#** in the key of A. The main character note of this scale is the D#. The D# creates the interesting dissonance as it is a #4th interval away from the tonic.

The formula for the Lydian Pentatonic scale is 1 3 #4 5 7.

When learning new scales, remember that sometimes they will sound unusual and possibly even dissonant to your ears at first. The further your ear develops, the more you will be able to appreciate these wonderful sounds.

The licks in this chapter work over an A Maj7#11 chord. You can also experiment using these licks over an A5 power chord if you prefer a rockier approach!

Shown below is the '**A Maj7#11**' chord. This beautiful sounding chord will work well underneath the licks in this chapter.

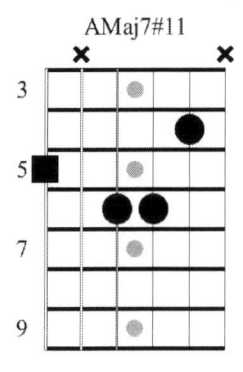

As well as an Amaj7#11, the licks in this chapter work well over Backing Track Four.

A Lydian Pentatonic – Position 1 'E' Shape

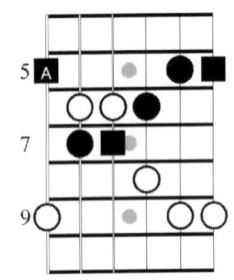

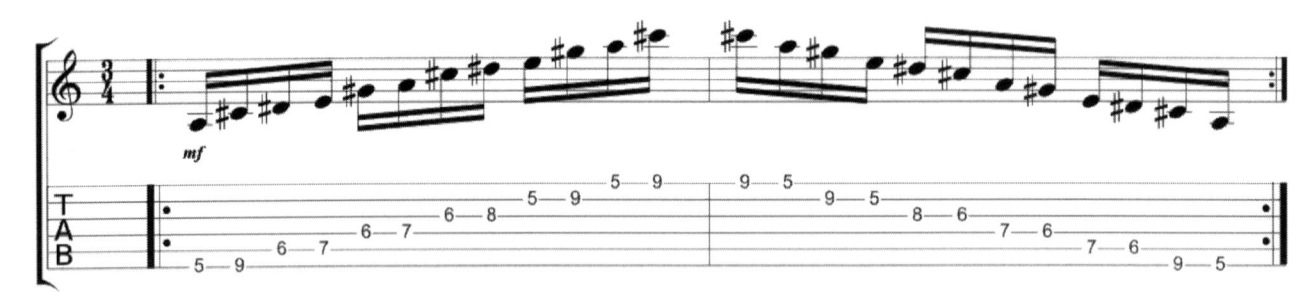

A Lydian Pentatonic
Position One

Example 9a includes a one-fret bend and creates an interesting 'Eastern' quality to the lick. The Lydian Pentatonic scale brings new life to major based progressions when used in place of the more common Major Pentatonic scale.

Example 9a

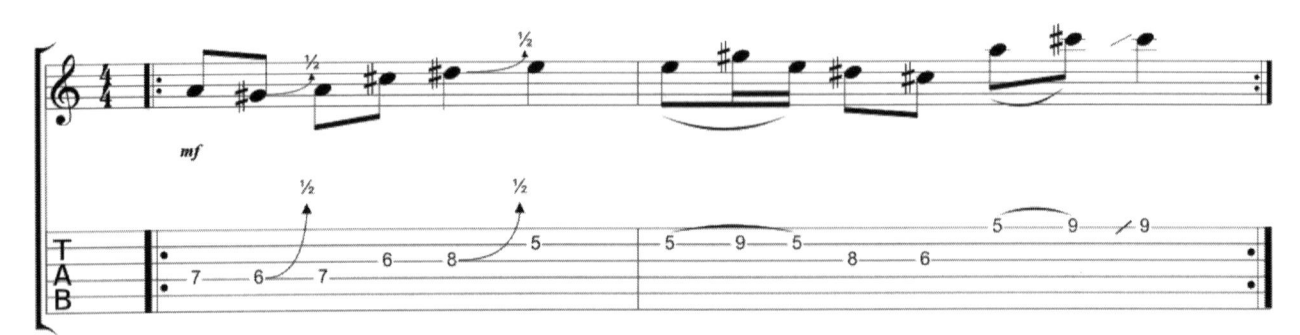

A Lydian Pentatonic – Position 2 'D' Shape

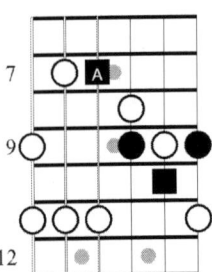

A Lydian Pentatonic
Position Two

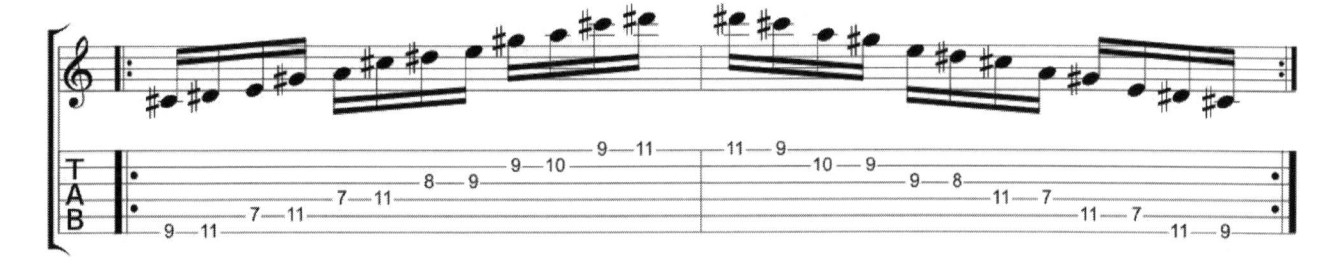

A common theme among Lydian Pentatonic licks is the bending of the note of D# up to E.

Try combining example 9a and example 9b, to create a longer Lydian pentatonic line.

Example 9b

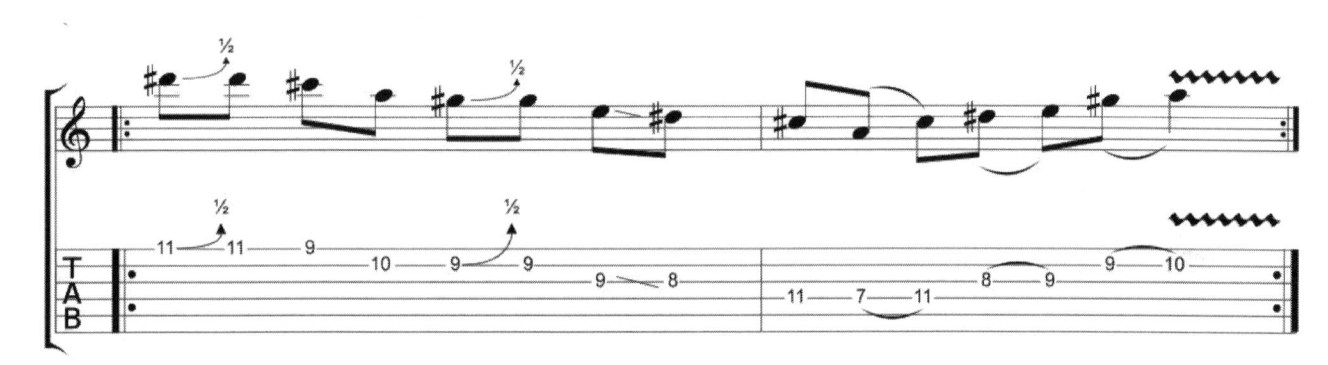

A Lydian Pentatonic – Position 3 'C' Shape

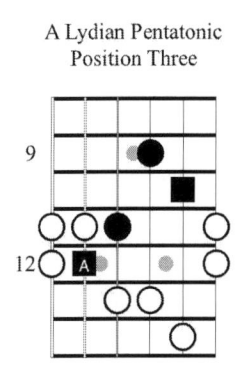

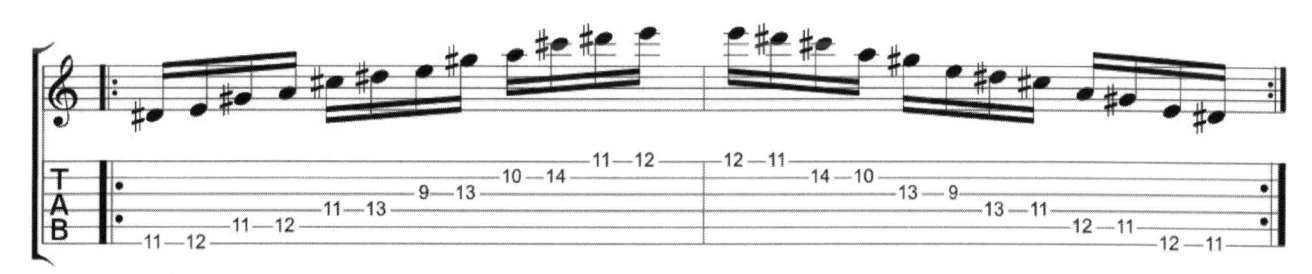

Example 9c demonstrates how to put together licks using a combination of upward and downward slides. The addition of alternate picking with the slides, and occasional string skip is what gives this lick its character. I like the unresolved nature of the lick, finishing on a 'G#' instead of the more obvious root note.

Example 9c

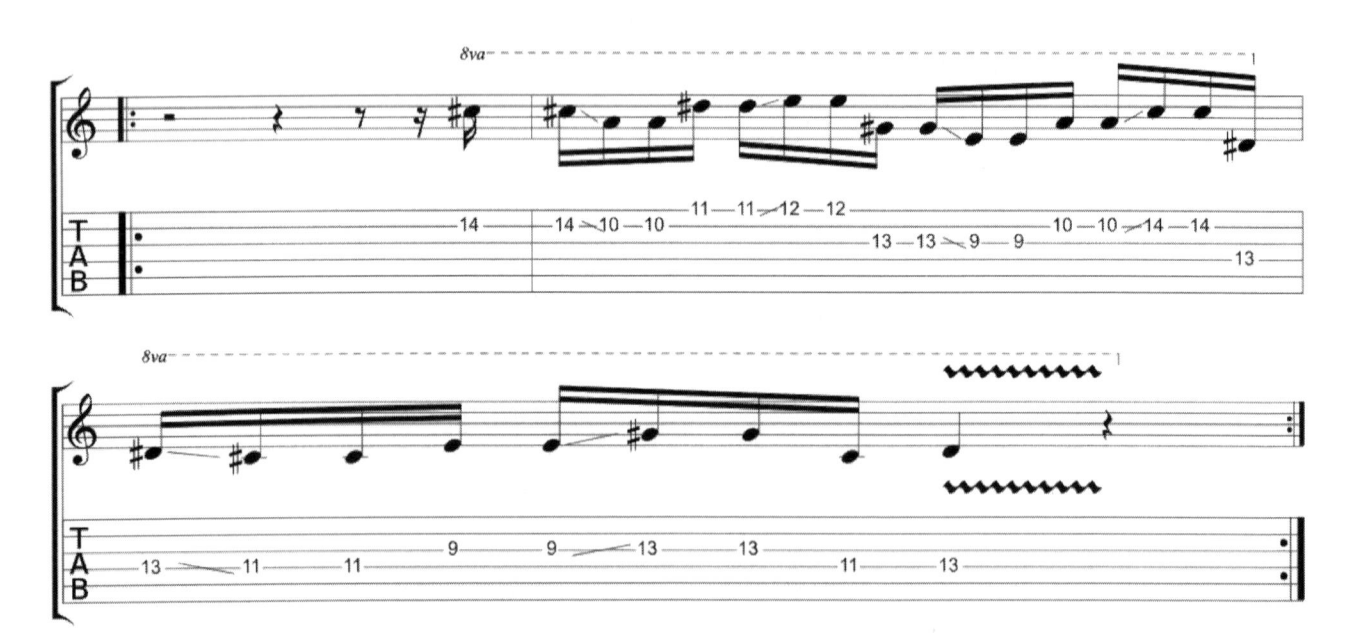

A Lydian Pentatonic – Position 4 'A' Shape

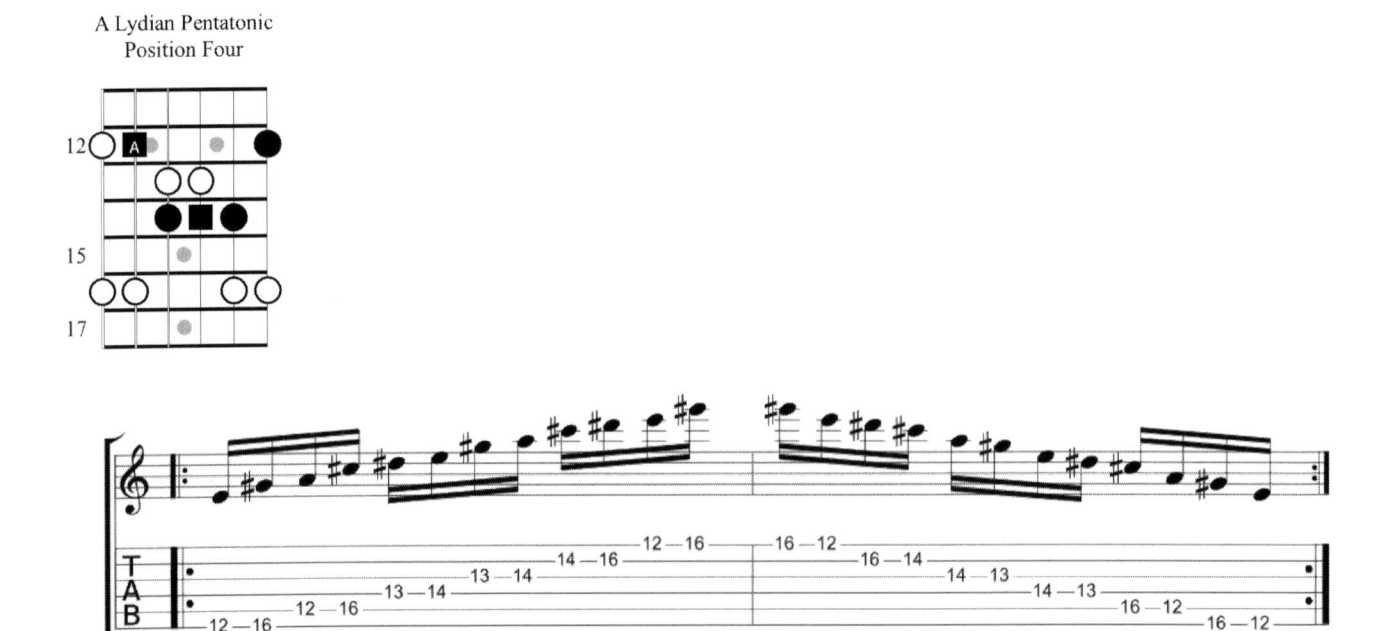

Example 9d is my favourite lick in this chapter. The repeating hammer-on and pull-off pattern interspersed with the ascending string skips in bar one will require some practice. As always, make sure you start slowly and don't rush to speed up the lick.

Bar two uses a one-fret bend once again, highlighting the dreamy quality this scale has to offer.

Example 9d

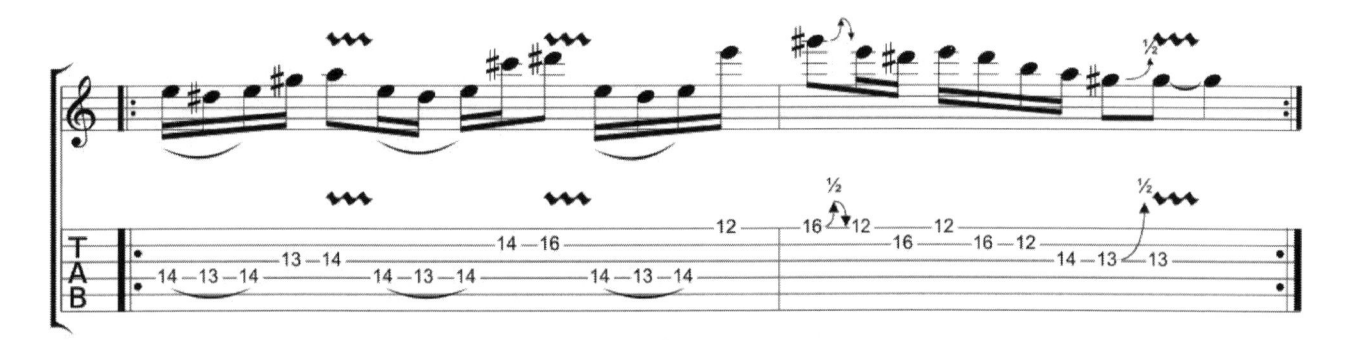

A Lydian Pentatonic – Position 5 'G' Shape

Example 9e incorporates a mixture of legato and alternate picking. It is fun to mix up your lead playing by combining the softer more fluid sound of legato with the harder more aggressive tone of alternate picking.

In bar two, we outline a mini pedal tone idea by alternating the A root note on the 3rd string with an ascending Lydian Pentatonic scale.

Example 9e

The licks demonstrated in this chapter are based on rock and jazz but can also create a dreamy Eastern feel. Backing Track Four works perfectly as an accompaniment to all the licks featured throughout this chapter.

When you start creating your own solos using the Lydian Pentatonic scale, remember that the dissonance of the scale is what makes it unique. Instead of 'perfectly resolved' soloing that we hear in commercial pop and rock music, you can always create Eastern-inspired ideas with modern rock techniques. Joe Satriani is a master of creating memorable melodies that have a Lydian dissonance at the very heart of them such as on the track Flying In A Blue Dream. Make sure to check out the discography at the end of the book to find artists who have inspired generations of guitar players.

If you are struggling to write your own ideas using the Lydian Pentatonic scale, be sure to use the techniques that were covered on page 20. By alternating between a lick you have already learnt and few bars of your own improvisation, you can build new ideas quickly and effectively.

Chapter Ten: The m7b5 Pentatonic Scale

Video: www.fundamental-changes.com/exotic-pentatonic-soloing   Password: hirojoshi

Backing Track Five

The Minor Seven Flat Five or 'Half Diminished' Pentatonic scale has a jazzy, modern sound to it. This scale is normally played over a m7b5 chord although it can create some interesting sounds on its own.

Guitarists who use this scale include Robben Ford and Larry Carlton. Both Ford and Carlton often play over complicated chord progressions and so look to find quick and easy ways to solo competently over the changes. Pentatonic scales be an easy way to create fluid lead lines over all sorts of harmony.

The m7b5 Pentatonic contains the notes of **A C D Eb G** in the key of A.

The formula for the m7b5 Pentatonic scale is 1 b3 4 b5 b7.

The licks in this chapter will fit perfectly over an Am7b5 chord, but also work perfectly with Backing Track Five.

The notes highlighted in black in this chapter are the underlying Am7b5 chord shapes.

Am7b5 Pentatonic – Position 1 'E' Shape

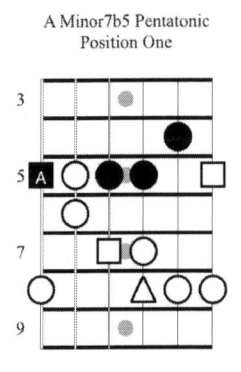

The triangle in this diagram is an alternative way to play the Eb on the 'B' string at the 4th fret. If you find this scale uncomfortable or hard to fret, try using the Eb at the 7th fret on the 'G' string instead of the Eb on the 2nd string.

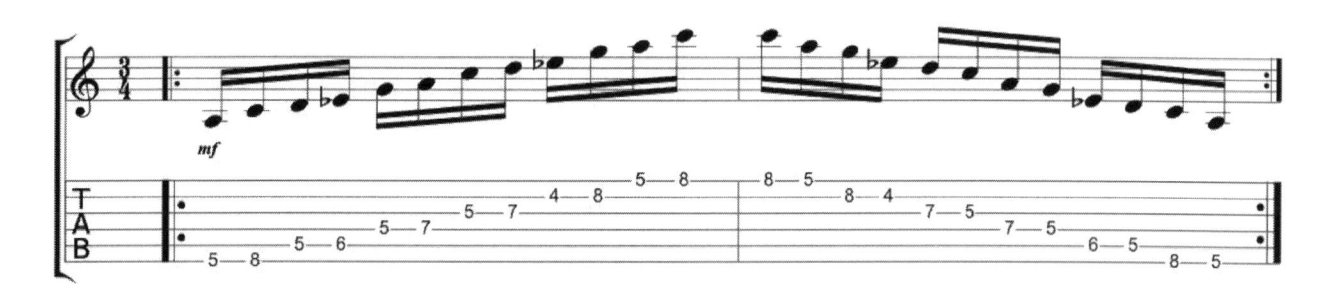

Fitting these intervals into a box-shape pentatonic pattern creates some slightly tricky fingerings. Take time to familiarise yourself with the scale shape and then train your fingers to know the pattern off by heart.

Example 10a demonstrates one angular sound that this scale can offer.

Example 10a

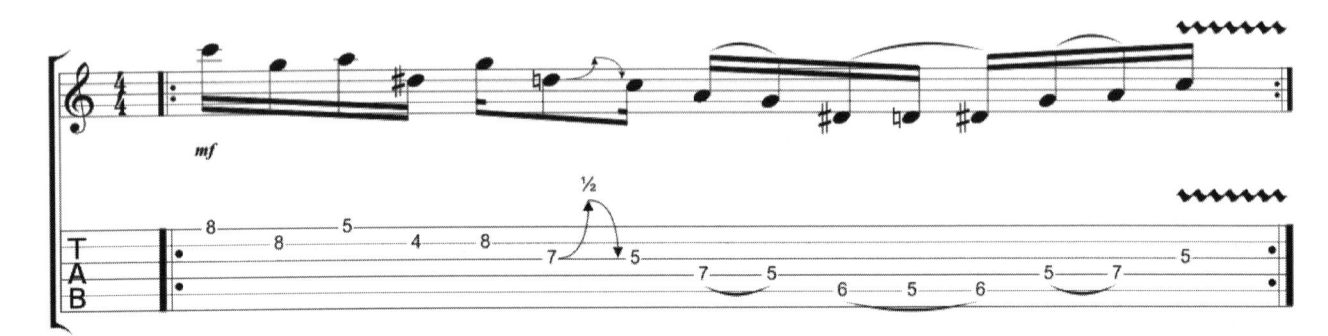

Am7b5 Pentatonic – Position 2 'D' Shape

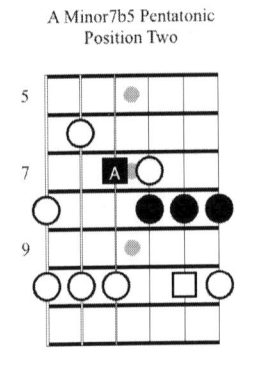

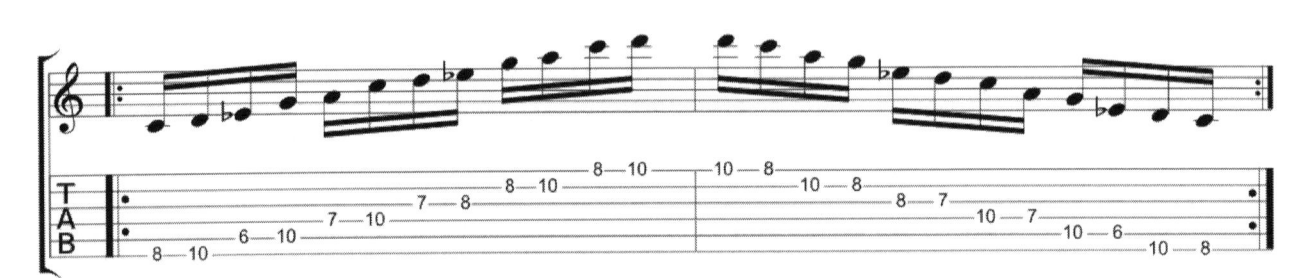

This lick has a modern jazz-fusion feel to it. Try using the m7b5 Pentatonic scale with modern rock techniques and a touch of distortion to see what fresh ideas you can create. If you are in doubt as to the best fingering to use in this lick, watch the corresponding video and see how I tackle it.

Example 10b

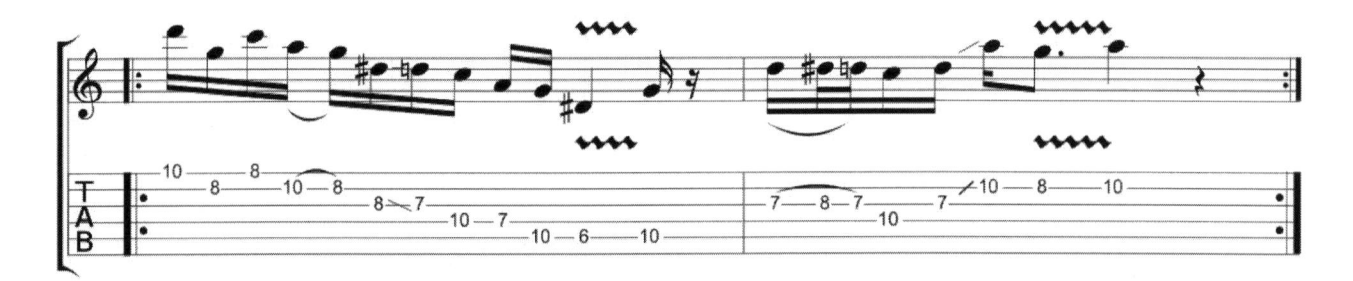

Am7b5 Pentatonic – Position 3 'C' Shape

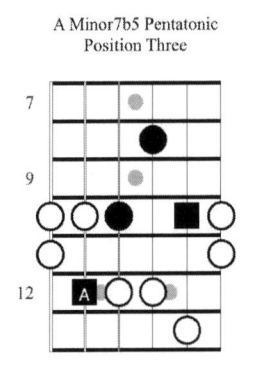

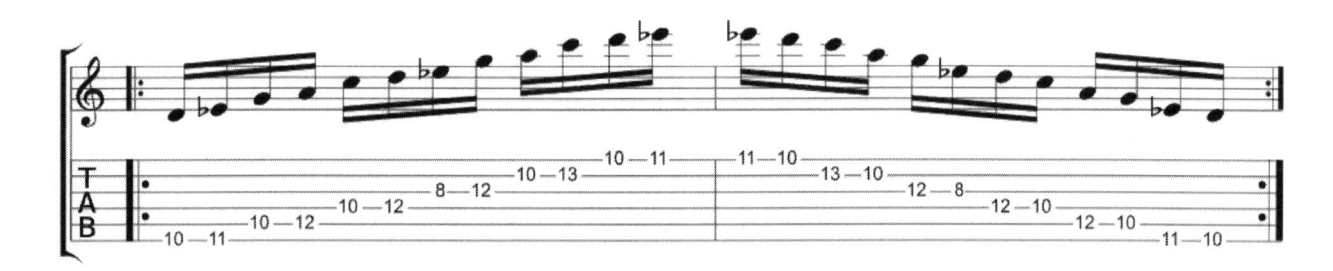

In this example, we start with a fun bending idea. Bending two strings at once sounds bluesy and incredibly raw. We use a blues curl on the E and B strings together to create a bluesy sound. Bar one is a complete lick on its own, and should be memorised and played in many different keys. Bar two resolves the lick with a combination of slides, bends and vibrato.

Example 10c

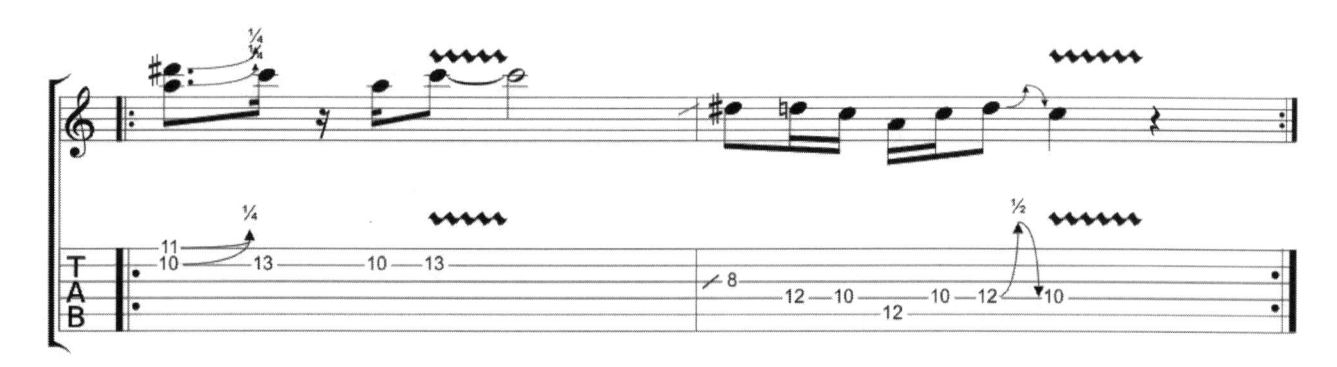

Am7b5 Pentatonic – Position 4 'A' Shape

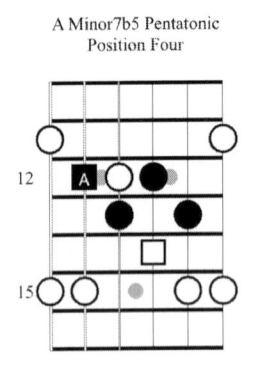

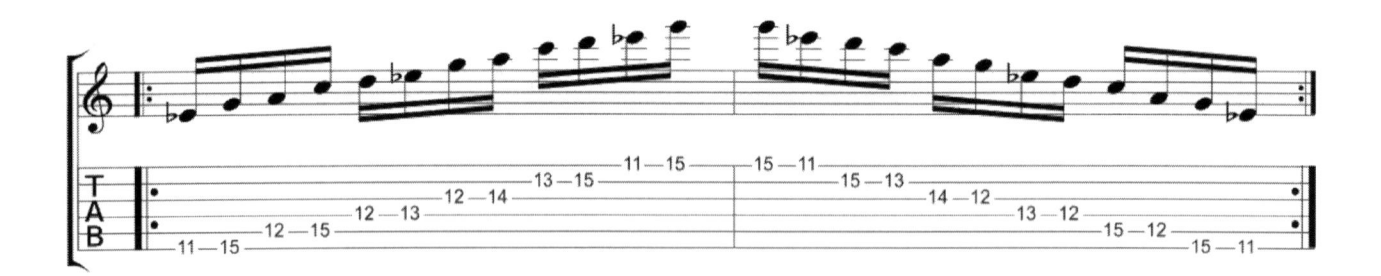

Example 10d is a legato-based pattern that uses a wide stretch on the top E string. This develops the coordination and strength of your fourth finger. I often like to write licks that work on areas of my playing that want to improve.

Example 10d

Am7b5 Pentatonic – Position 5 'G' Shape

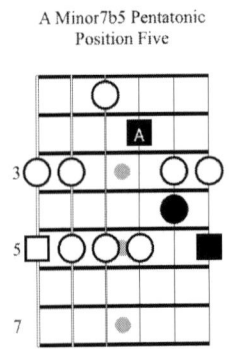

60

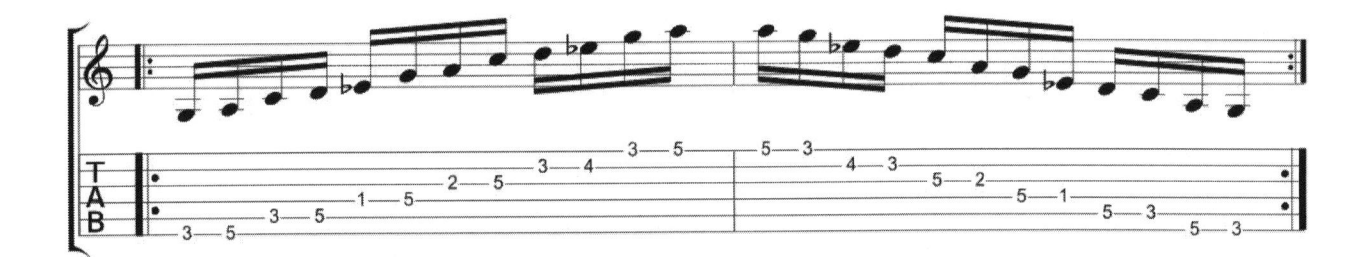

Example 10e introduces a dissonant 'jazz' idea. One creative way to use pentatonic scales is to imagine that you are writing music for different scenarios. This lick could be used as a theme for a horror film or a fight scene in a video game. Think about how many situations involve music; adverts, films, TV, video games and online media all need music in a wide variety of genres.

A technique I like to use is to create a piece of music (or lick) based on certain imagery. For example, imagine a hot-air balloon ride; try creating the wind and the sound of the flame using a combination of techniques and melody. You can use bends, slides, hammer-ons, pull-offs and vibrato to conjure up the musical illusion of the setting you are trying to convey.

Example 10e

The examples featured in this chapter have a jazz and blues fusion vibe, and work extremely well over Backing Track Five. The backing track itself is a one-chord vamp, meaning that the Am7b5 chord is continuous throughout the track. You can also use this scale over Backing Track Six too.

A lot of blues and rock players feel daunted by the prospect of playing jazz. By applying licks and ideas learnt in this chapter (especially example 10b), you can ease yourself into jazzier tones without any thought of advanced theory.

One main difference between blues licks and jazz licks is that jazz licks tend to not contain any bent notes. As example 10b demonstrates, slides, hammer-ons and pull-offs and note targeting are the main options when creating a jazz-fusion line.

Try using example 10b as the basis for a new jazzy improvisation. Put on Backing Track Five and alternate between two bars of example 10b and two bars of your own improvisation. When you feel comfortable with that, experiment with the other licks in this chapter and combine them in any way you see fit.

Remember, "If it sounds good; it is!"

Chapter Eleven: The Maj7#5 Pentatonic Scale

Video: www.fundamental-changes.com/exotic-pentatonic-soloing   Password: hirojoshi

Backing Track Six

The 'Major Seven Sharp 5' Pentatonic scale has a modern jazz tonality. This scale is predominantly used to accompany a 'Maj7#5' chord, but can create interesting sounds on its own as well. The E# (F) note here is the focal point of the scale. This note 'wants' to resolve to E, but left unresolved it sounds eerie and dissonant. This dissonance can be put to good use in modern styles such as fusion and jazz.

Guitarists such as Joe Pass and John Mclaughlin incorporate the Maj7#5 sound into their playing. They both often use unusual chord voicings and find appropriate scales to play over them.

The Maj7#5 Pentatonic contains the notes of **A C# D E# (F) G#** in the key of A.

The formula for the Maj7#5 Pentatonic scale is 1 3 4 #5 7.

The Maj7#5 chord contains the notes of A C# E# G#. You can see that we have simply added the note D here to create a new pentatonic scale shape. The licks in this chapter will fit perfectly over an A Maj7#5 chord. You can also use Backing Track Six to practice the licks in this chapter.

Top Tip

Invest some time listening to new genres and artists. Don't just restrict yourself to guitar-based artists either! Try saxophone players, violinists, vocalists. *Emulate, copy and steal as much as you possibly can from every source!*

The notes highlighted in black in this chapter are the underlying AMaj7#5 chord shapes.

A Major7#5 Pentatonic scale – Position 1 'E' Shape

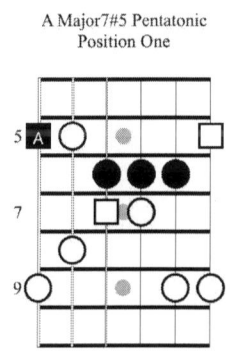

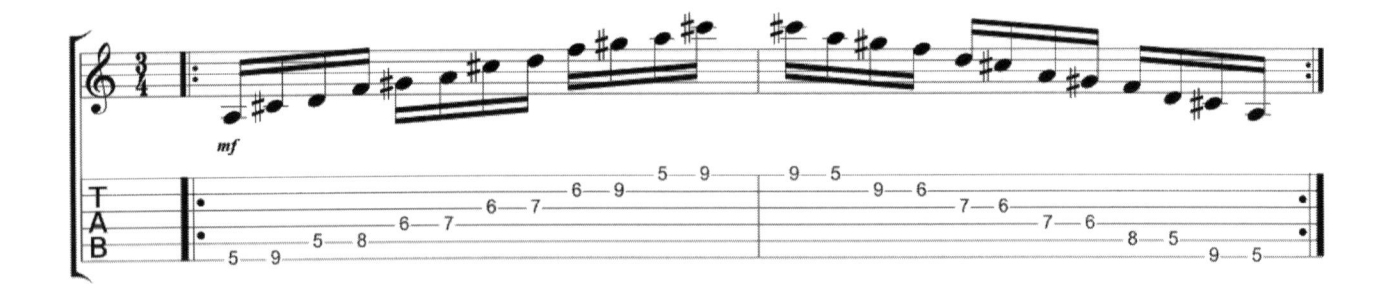

Example 11a is a repeated theme around an unusual melodic line. The Major 7#5 pentatonic is often used in film scores and it can be fantastically tense. The notes involved in this pentatonic shape do require you to learn a slightly less convenient fingering pattern.

Example 11a

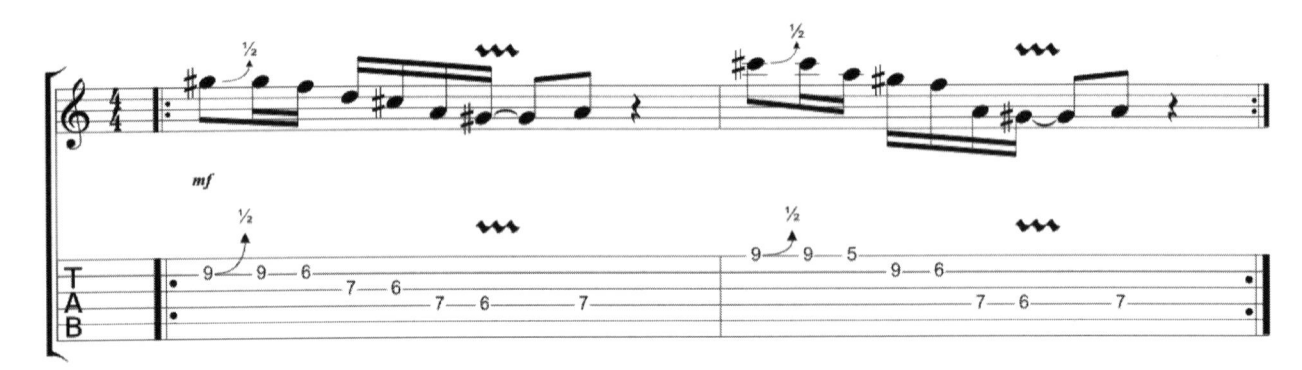

A Major7#5 Pentatonic – Position 2 'D' Shape

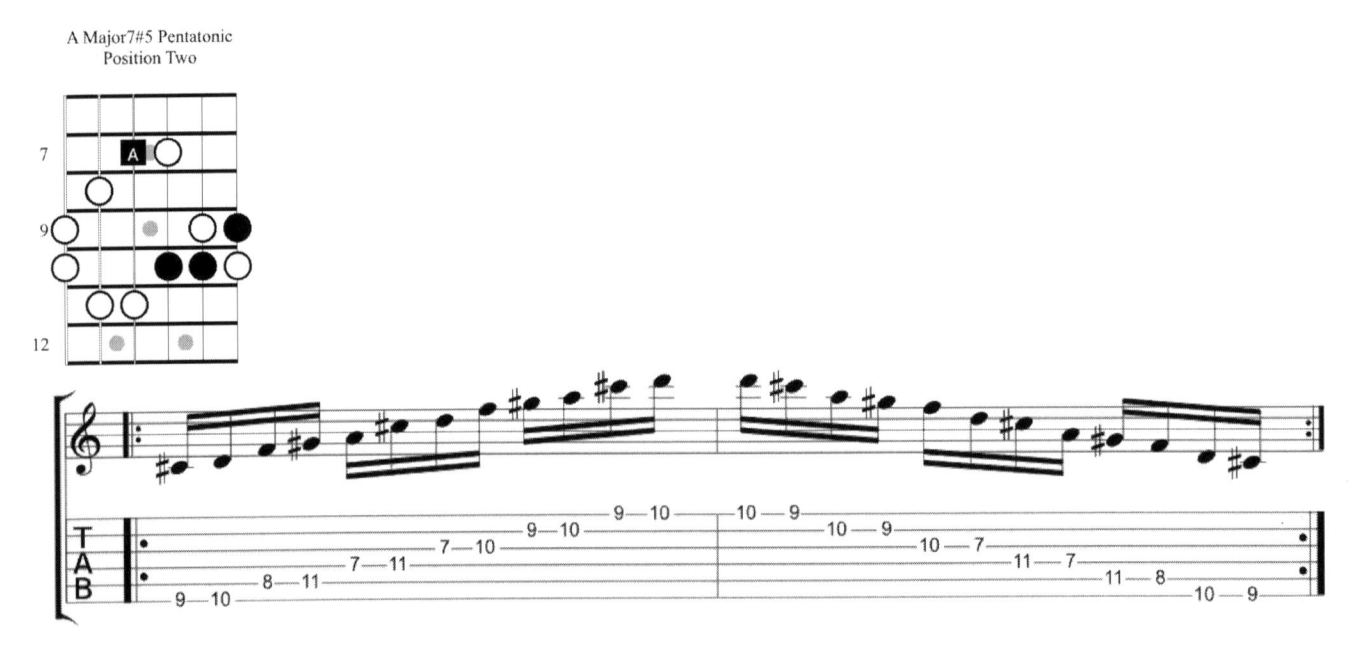

Example 11b again creates a jazz-based theme using only slides and alternate picking. The one technique you don't hear too frequently in jazz is bending, however, sometimes in gypsy jazz there are occasionally one-fret bends.

Example 11b

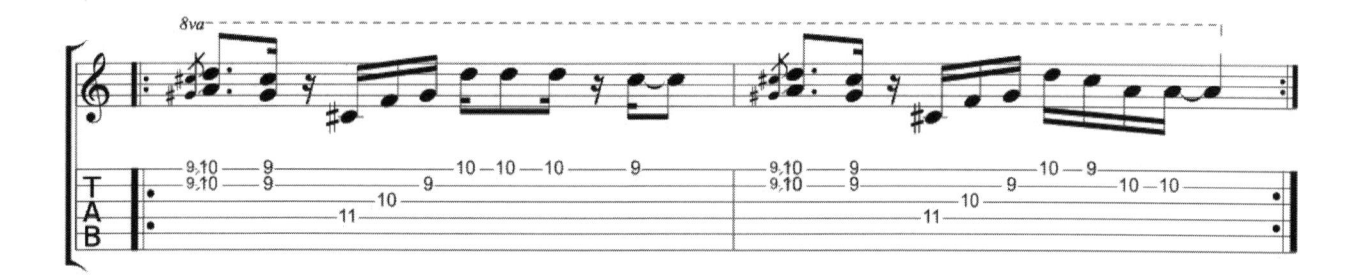

A Major7#5 Pentatonic – Position 3 'C' Shape

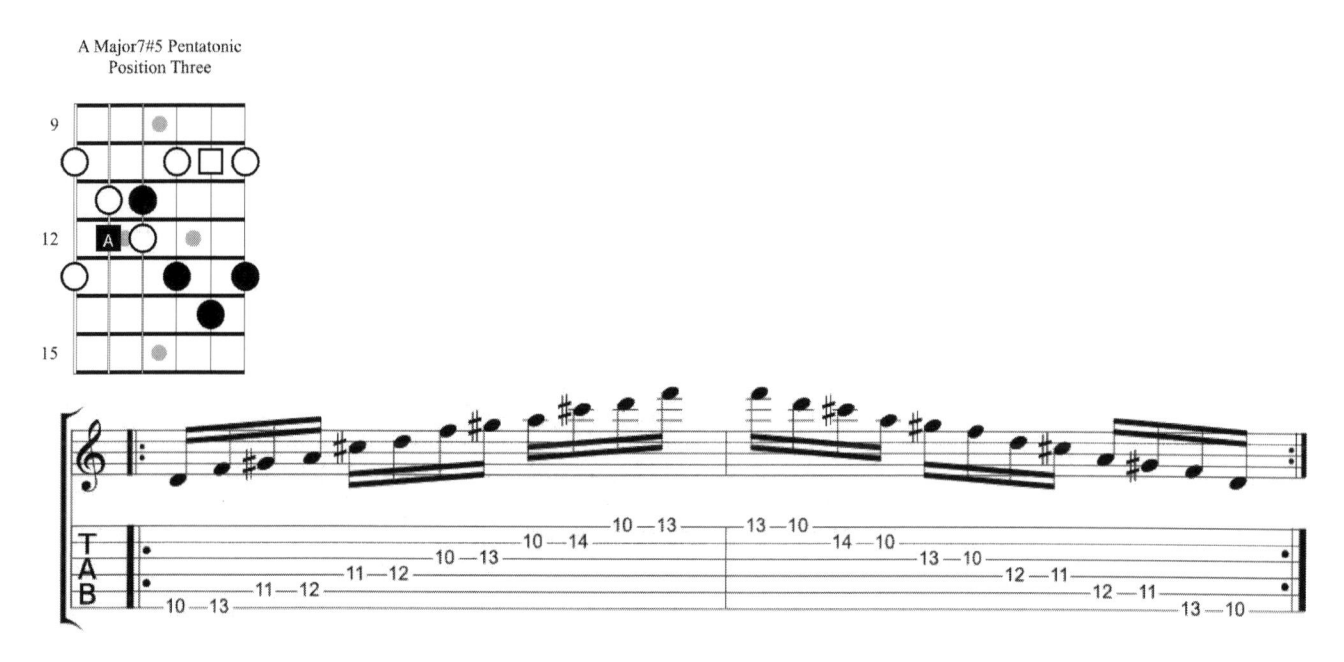

Example 11c shows a modern rock/metal alternate picking lick. The dissonance created in this lick is very popular with modern metal bands and is seen frequently in their rhythm guitar parts.

Try recording an A5 power chord and play this lick over the top of it to create a modern 'Nu-metal' sound.

Example 11c

A Major7#5 Pentatonic – Position 4 'A' Shape

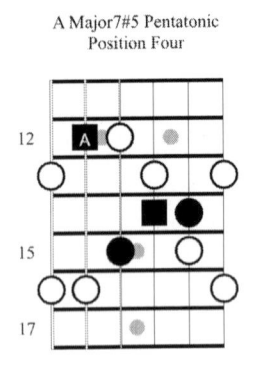

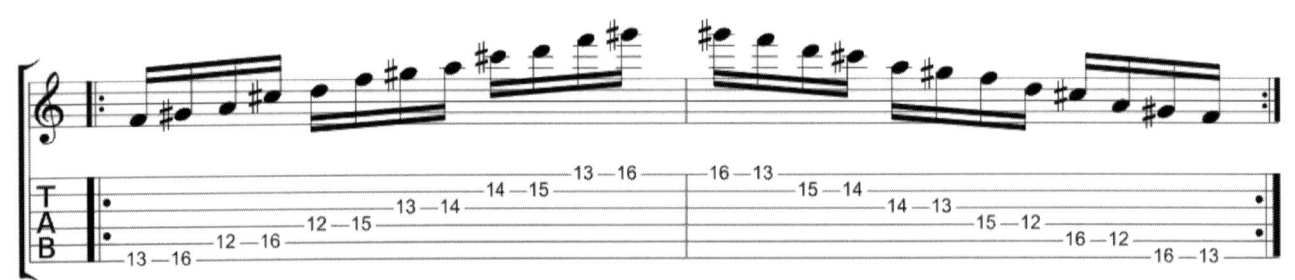

It's funk time! Adding mutes to a lick adds a nuance that is common in rhythm guitar but often overlooked in lead guitar playing.

Example 11d

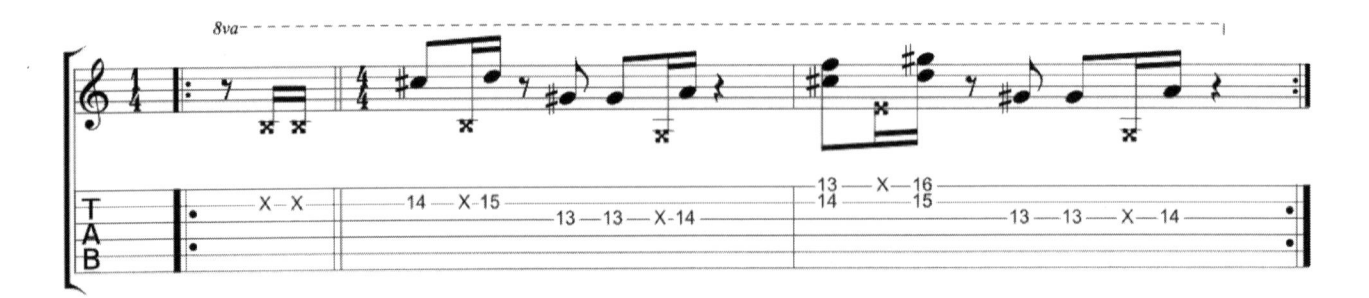

A Major7#5 Pentatonic – Position 5 'G' Shape

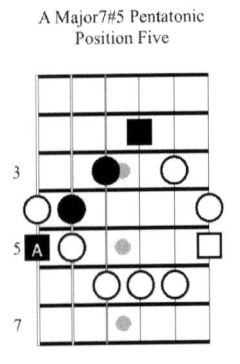

[Musical notation and tablature]

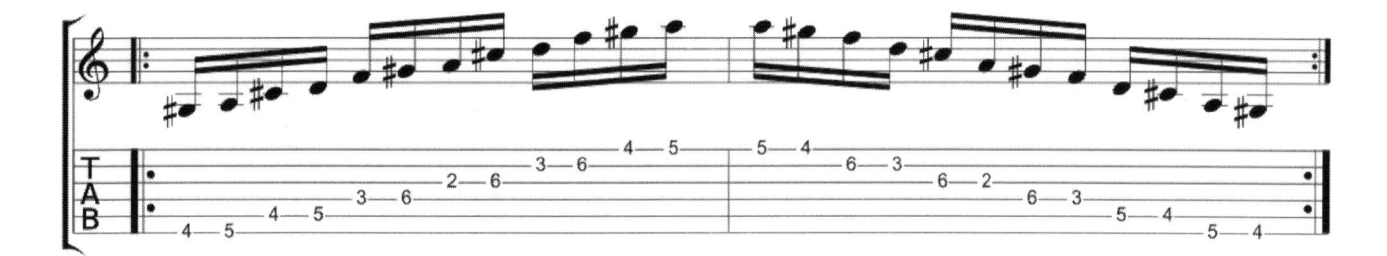

In this example, I took the liberty of allowing the open A string to act as a ringing drone note. Using an open string enables you to place all sorts of weird and wonderful notes over the top of it.

I highly recommend you try this with all the Pentatonic shapes in this book: Play an open A note and see what cool-sounding chords you can create, just from the pentatonic scales used in this book.

Example 11e

[Musical notation and tablature with "let ring" markings]

The licks in this chapter contain jazz, funk, blues and rock tones and fit over Backing Track Six. You will have noticed that the Backing Track Six is the most commonly used track throughout the whole book and every single lick and scale from this book can be played over it.

As well as practicing licks from individual chapters over specific backing tracks, try picking your favourites and play them back to back over Backing Track Six. This system of playing different scales with the same root note is called *Pitch Axis,* and is a technique that modern rock guitarists like Joe Satriani and Steve Vai often use.

By having a constant root note playing on the backing track and using a variety of different scale ideas, we now have a vast array of musical colours we can use.

An example of a timeline using pitch axis is shown below.

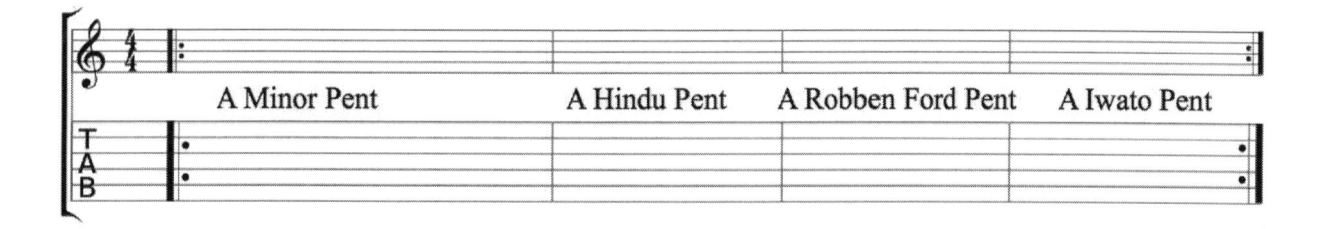

[Musical staff in 4/4 with labels: A Minor Pent | A Hindu Pent | A Robben Ford Pent | A Iwato Pent]

Shown above is a simple diagram showing how you could use four different licks from four chapters of this book over Backing Track Six.

Chapter Twelve: The Iwato Pentatonic Scale

Video: www.fundamental-changes.com/exotic-pentatonic-soloing Password: hirojoshi

Backing Track Six

The final two chapters of this book introduce some more 'Eastern' sounds. My aim here is to try to bring a touch of the East into your playing style.

The Iwato Pentatonic scale is used in traditional Japanese music. Japanese music often uses pentatonic scales, making it a prime candidate for study.

Marty Friedman is an expert at soloing using exotic Eastern sounding scales. He blends them with rock techniques to create his unique sound. I recommend watching and listening to Friedman's Scenes album to hear how new scale sounds can be used.

The Iwato Pentatonic scale contains the notes **A Bb D Eb G** in the key of A. The note of Bb provides the initial dissonance, which is then reinforced by the Eb. The scale has a dark, minor tonality and works well with modern rock metal techniques.

The formula for the Iwato Pentatonic scale is 1 b2 4 b5 b7.

Backing Track Six works perfectly for the ideas in this chapter as it gives you a blank canvas with which to improvise. When using exotic scales it is often a good idea to keep the melodic content of the backing track/song simple. This allows you to solo using the new tonality without worrying about possible clashes. Backing Track Six is a one-note groove in the style of guitarists like Joe Satriani or Marty Friedman.

Although the licks in this chapter do fit around the CAGED Am, shapes, these are a little more difficult to see so I have highlighted only the root notes as your guides.

A Iwato Pentatonic – Position 1 'E' Shape

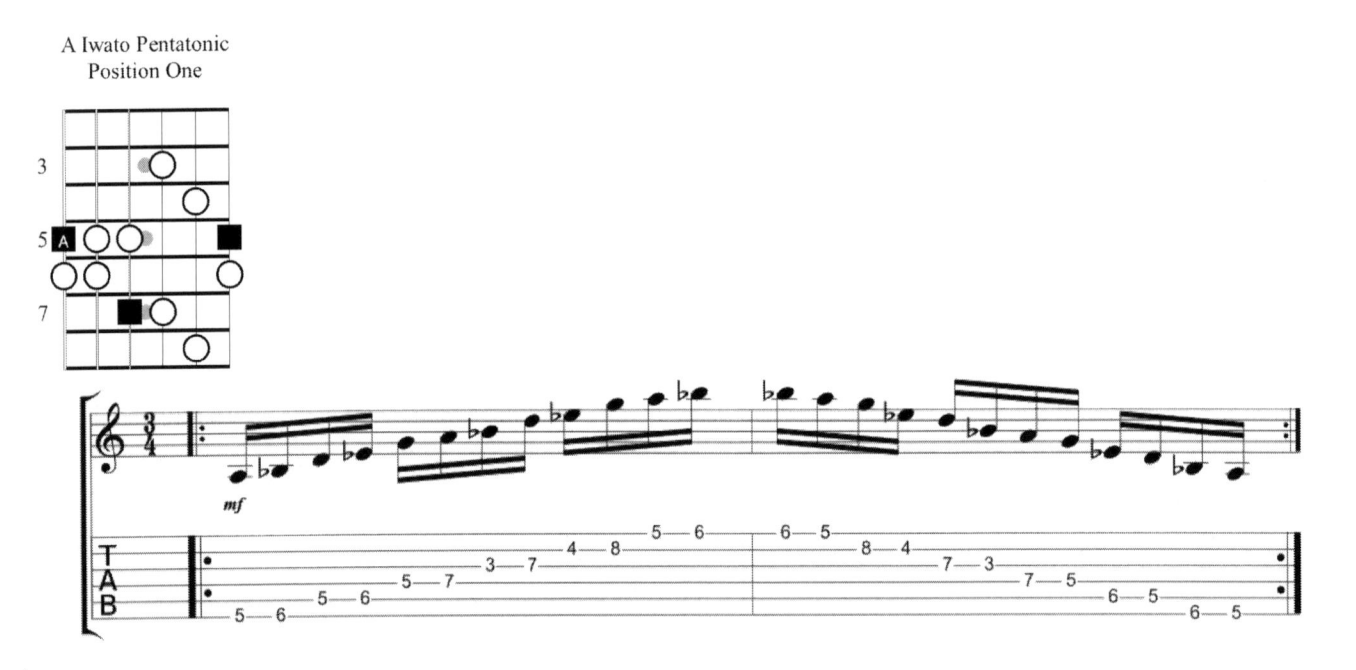

By using octave patterns instead of single note ideas, riffs sound fuller and fatter. It is normally easier to write licks using single notes first, and then add in octave shape after you have created the melody.

Sliding octaves is more technically challenging than playing each shape individually however the resulting sound is well worth the practice.

Example 12a

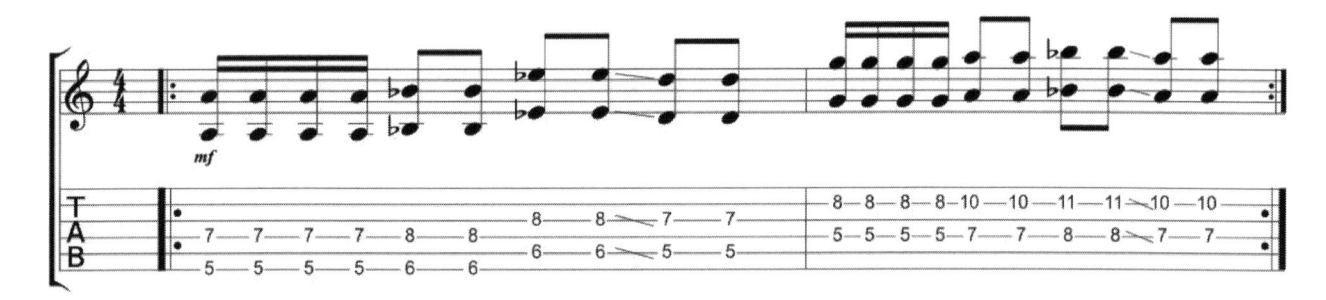

A Iwato Pentatonic – Position 2 'D' Shape

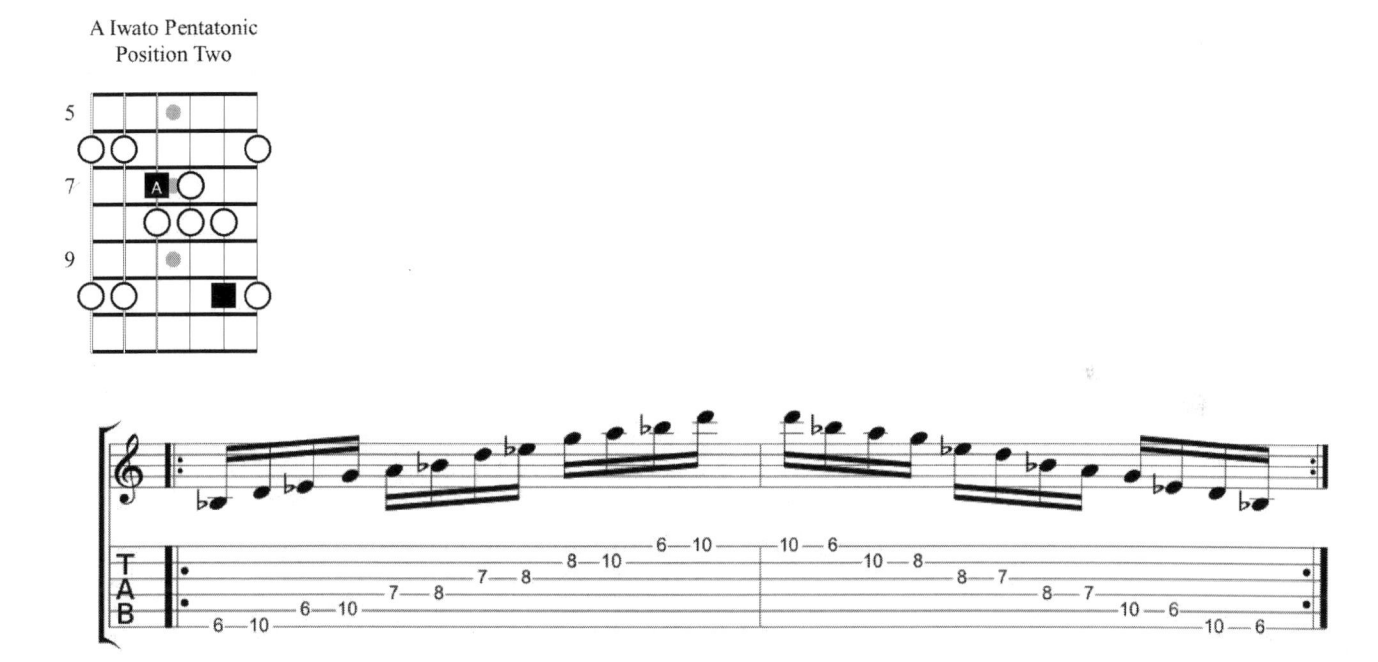

Example 12b is both a melodic line and a complex technical lick. The first two bars create a delicate, Eastern-flavoured melody based around a single-string line. Often, restricting yourself to just one string, forces you to create melodic lines by limiting the notes available.

Bars three and four use a string-skipping legato pattern; Paul Gilbert loves to arrange his arpeggios like this. Check out the corresponding video to see how I mute the strings, giving me freedom to concentrate on melodic expression.

The best way to practice muting is to crank up the distortion on your amp when you play. This way, you can hear any unwanted buzzing and fret or string noise. Try to counteract any unwanted noise by muting with both hands where appropriate.

Example 12b

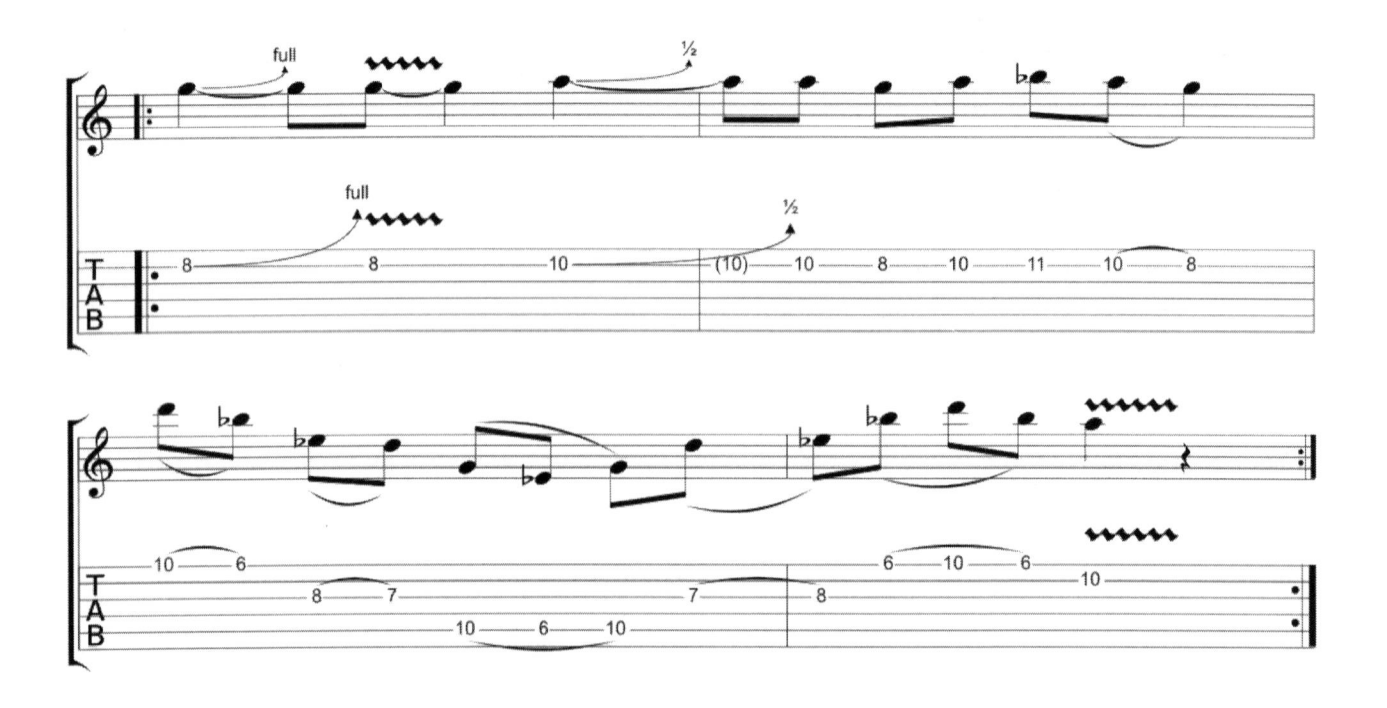

A Iwato Pentatonic – Position 3 'C' Shape

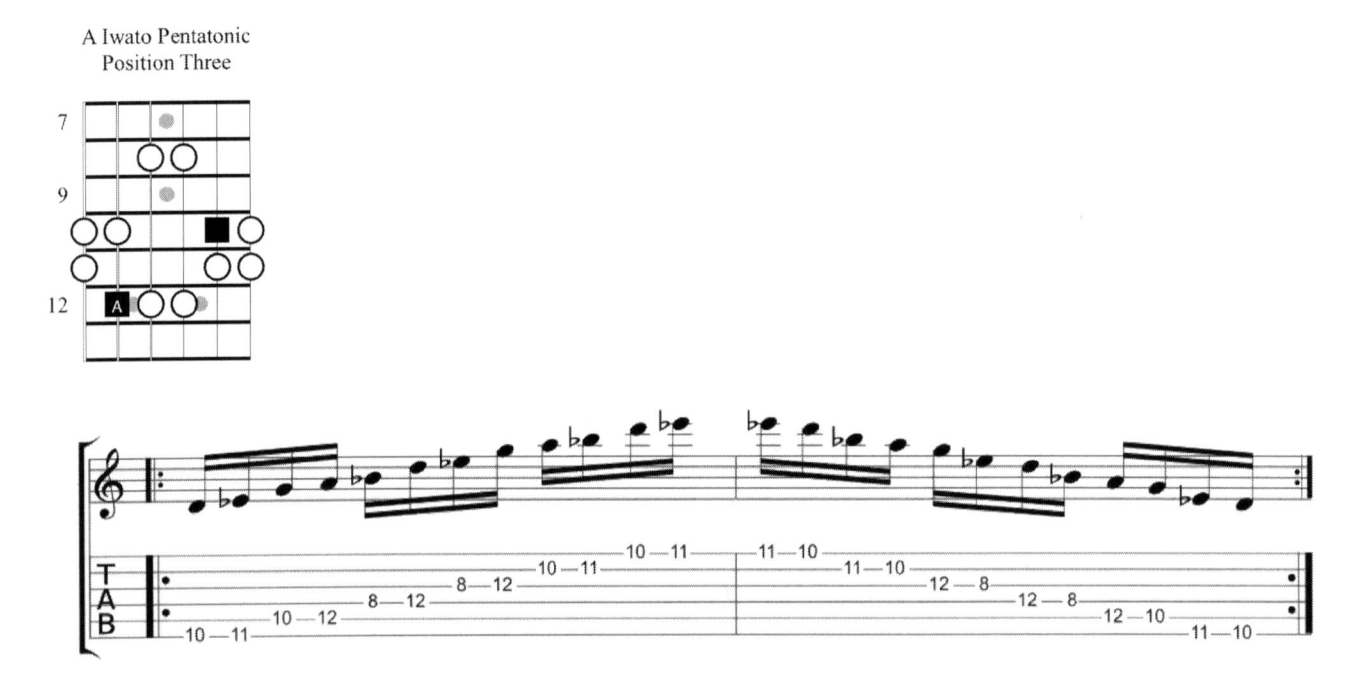

This example introduces a two-tone bend and bending the equivalent of four frets is a hard skill to master. Play the note you are targeting before attempting the bend to make sure you are always bending in tune.

Lighter string gauges such as 0.09s are easier to bend than heavier gauges such as 0.012s.

Example 12c

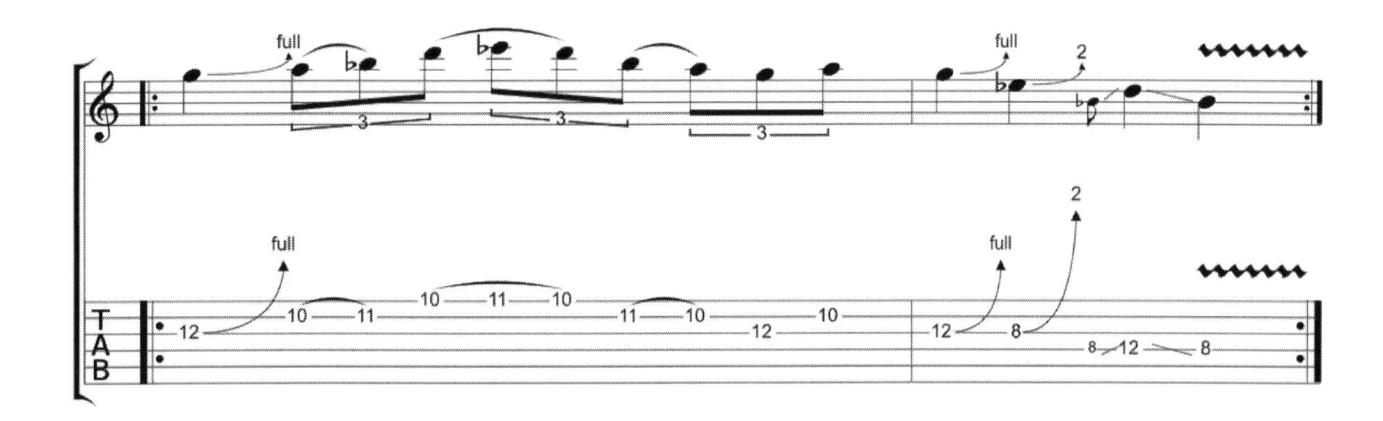

A Iwato Pentatonic – Position 4 'A' Shape

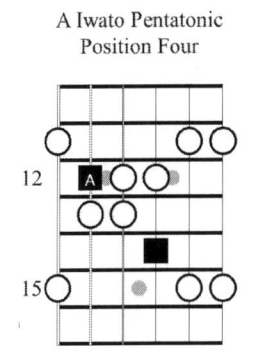

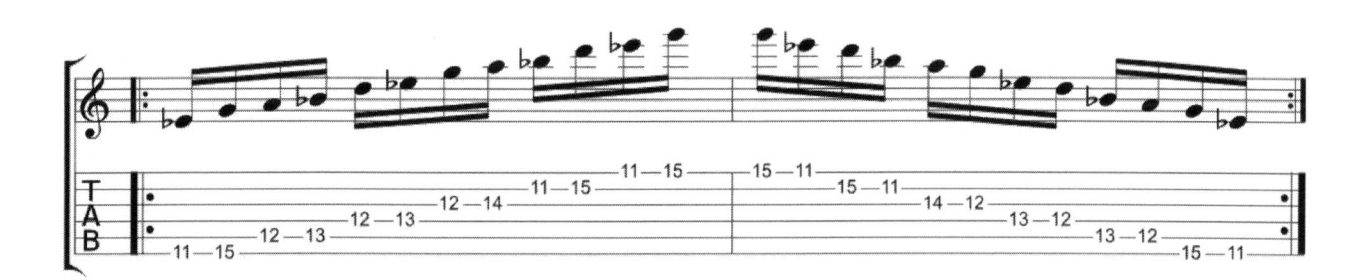

In example 12d, we see how descending triplet patterns can work well when creating modern-sounding rock lead lines. I enjoy combining modern techniques with Eastern-sounding scales and made this example part of my daily practice regime.

Make sure that your pick strokes are the same volume as your hammer-ons and pull-offs unless you want to accent certain notes for melodic effect.

Example 12d

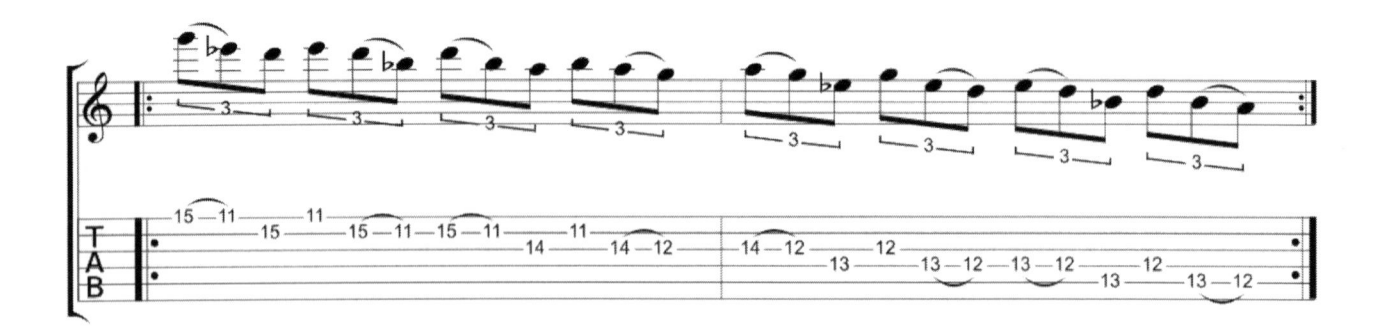

A Iwato Pentatonic – Position 5 'G' Shape

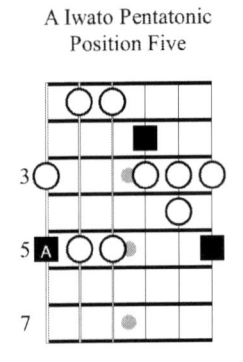

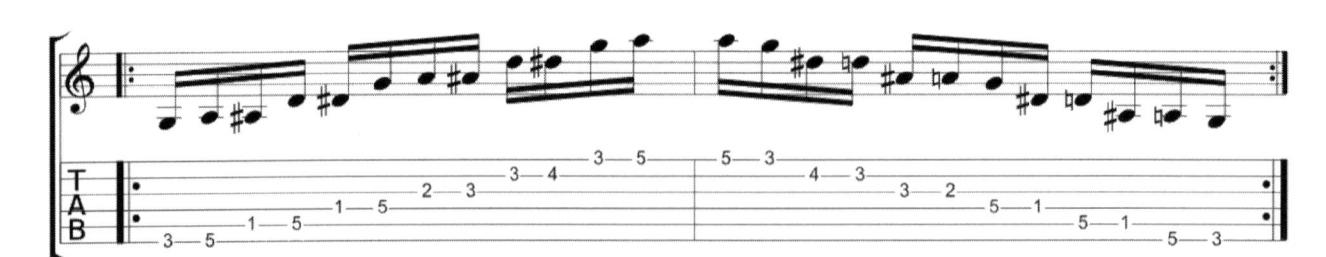

Django Reinhardt makes an unexpected appearance here. An incredibly effective technique is to use his 'hammer-on, pull-off, slide, slide' technique. This technique can make even a couple of notes sound sophisticated. Modern rock metal players copy this sound and use it with different scale patterns. Try creating your own licks using this new idea.

Example 12e

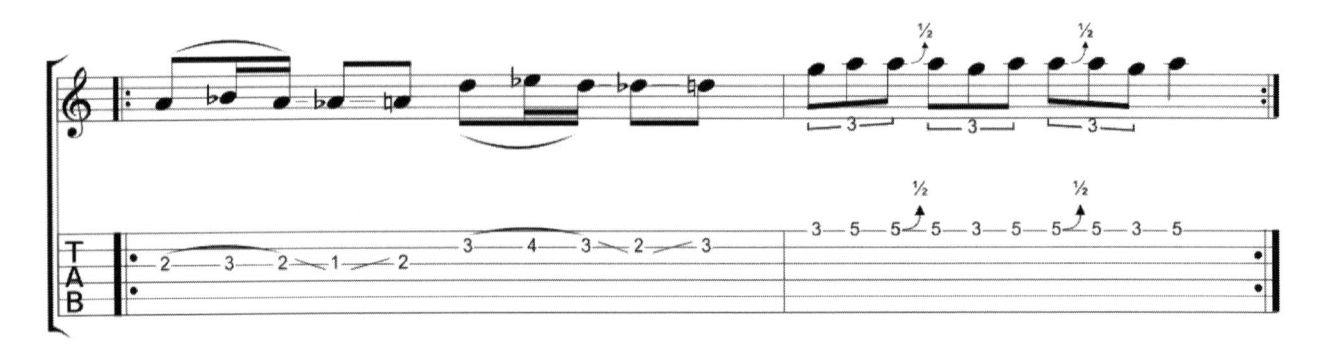

The licks demonstrated in this chapter have an 'Eastern rock' feel, and Backing Track Six is the perfect accompaniment for them. Even though the Iwato Pentatonic scale comes from traditional Japanese folk music, it works very well with modern rock guitar techniques.

Example 12b introduced string skips into your lick vocabulary. By creating licks that use non-adjacent strings we are able to add excitement with intervallic leaps.

A IWATO PENTATONIC - Using E, D and B Strings

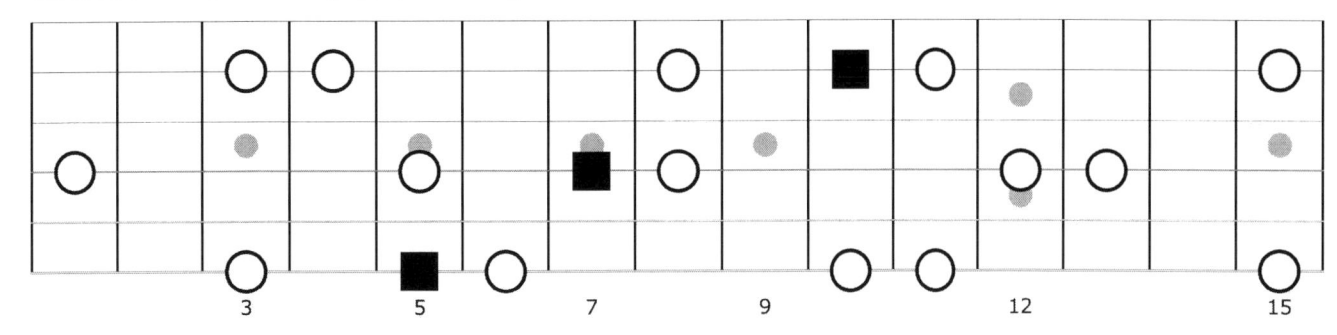

Shown above are the notes of the Iwato Pentatonic scale, but only on the E, D and B strings. The fantastic thing about arranging the notes like this is that it forces you to play outside of your comfort zone. Not only will the notes shown here help your lead guitar playing, they will also improve your fretboard knowledge.

By learning scale shapes both linearly and non-linearly you will be able to create solos that are not confined to box patterns and shapes.

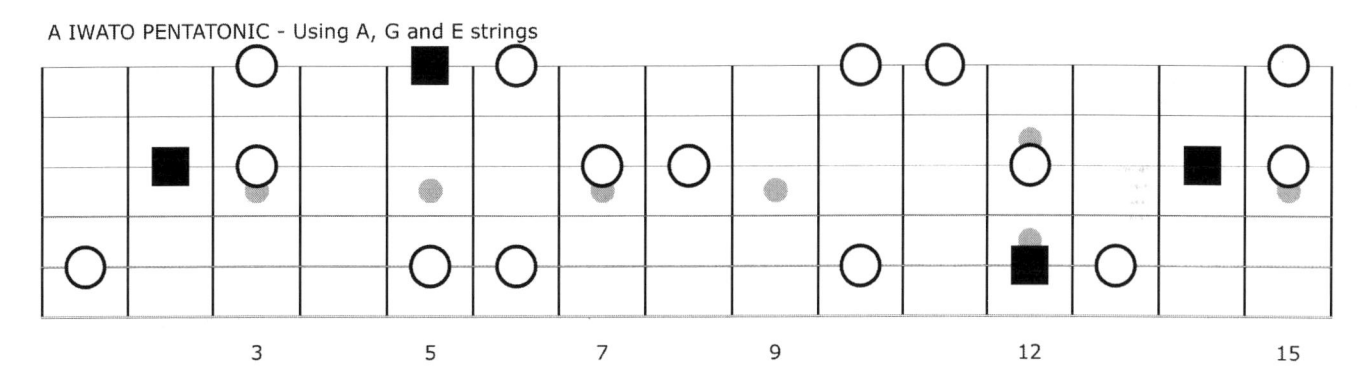

A IWATO PENTATONIC - Using A, G and E strings

The above diagram shows the Iwato pentatonic through five positions, but only using the A, G and high E strings.

Top tip!

By now, you are probably swimming in a sea of new ideas and possibilities. I recommend you create your own personal video lick book for reference. Film your licks, and if possible write them out in standard notation or tab. That way, when you look back in six months time, not only can you see and hear how far your playing has come, you can revisit licks that you may have forgotten.

Chapter Thirteen: The Hirojoshi Pentatonic Scale

Video: www.fundamental-changes.com/exotic-pentatonic-soloing Password: hirojoshi

Backing Track Six

The Hirojoshi Pentatonic scale has a Japanese sound and works well with modern electric guitar techniques. Traditionally, stringed instruments such as the Koto were used to play these interesting-sounding scales. These five note Japanese scales lend themselves well to the five CAGED shapes on the guitar.

Modern-day Japanese pop music has become more commercialised and now bears more resemblance to western music although more traditional Japanese music still contains the favours and sounds of its early heritage.

The Hirojoshi Pentatonic contains the notes of **A B C E F** in the key of A.

The formula for the Hirojoshi Pentatonic scale is 1 2 b3 5 b6.

Big intervallic gaps often lead to unusual patterns on the guitar and the Hirojoshi Pentatonic combines both big and small intervals to create its unique sound. As always, make sure you study each shape in detail and memorise each pattern before diving into all the licks. Once again, the Hirojoshi Pentatonic scale works best over Backing Track Six.

Top Tip!

Don't Restrict Yourself! The guitar is one of the most expressive and adaptable instruments on earth. Try listening to styles of music you would never have imagined yourself enjoying. Japanese folk music is probably not high on your list of priority listening, but after engaging with it, you may be able to develop exciting new ideas to spice up your music.

Shown below is a simple A5 power chord. This power chord works extremely well under the Eastern-flavoured licks in this chapter.

Although the licks in this chapter do fit around the CAGED A minor shapes, just the root notes are highlighted for reference.

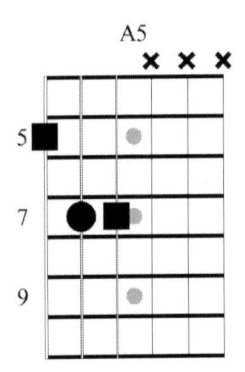

A Hirojoshi Pentatonic – Position 1 'E' Shape

The first lick immediately highlights the sound of the Hirojoshi Pentatonic scale. In bars one and two, the lick revolves around a repeated one fret bending theme. Bar three is a little trickier to fret, with the A root note used as a pedal tone during the ascending bends. Use the one-finger-per-fret rule where possible, but if this feels unnatural, go with whatever works for you. In Eastern music, dissonant double-stops are often used; and this can be heard at the end of the third bar.

Example 13a

A Hirojoshi Pentatonic – Position 2 'D' Shape

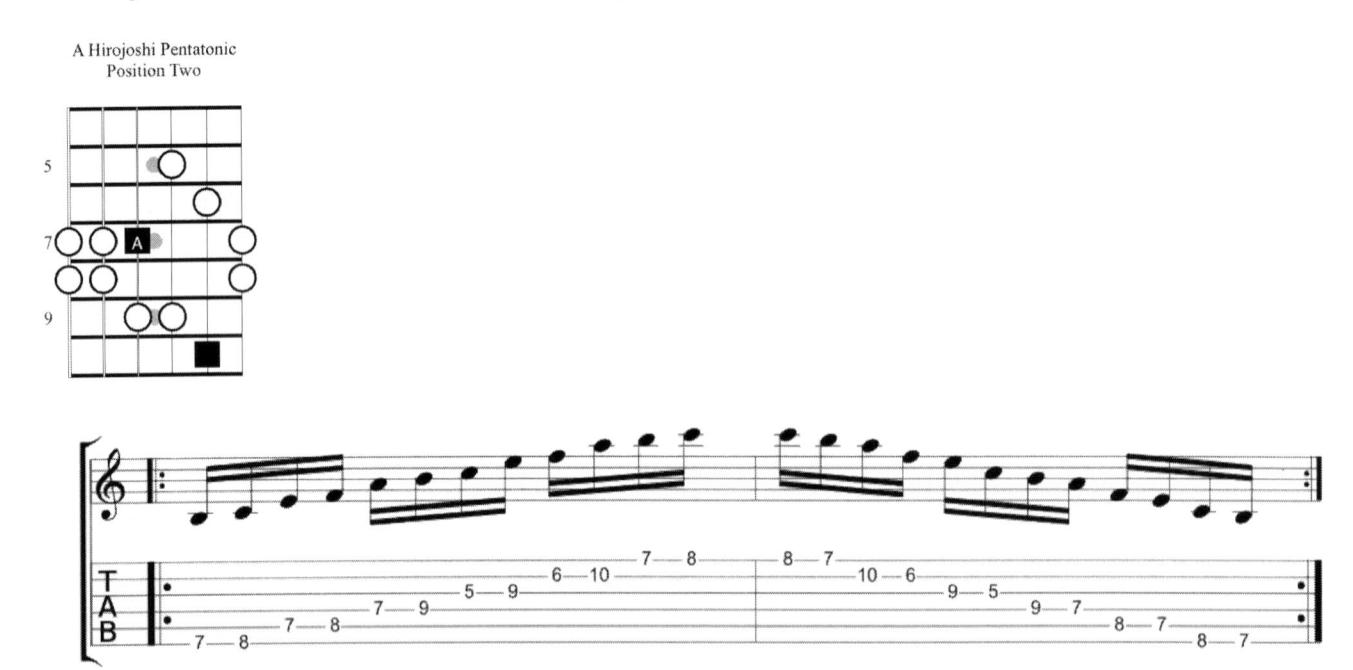

In bar one there is a simple bending theme that uses both two-fret, and three-fret bends. Resolving these bends back to the A root note makes the listener aware of where home is. Bar two is reminiscent of some Marty Friedman-style rock licks. He uses flowing legato lines to create his unique Eastern rock sound.

Example 13b

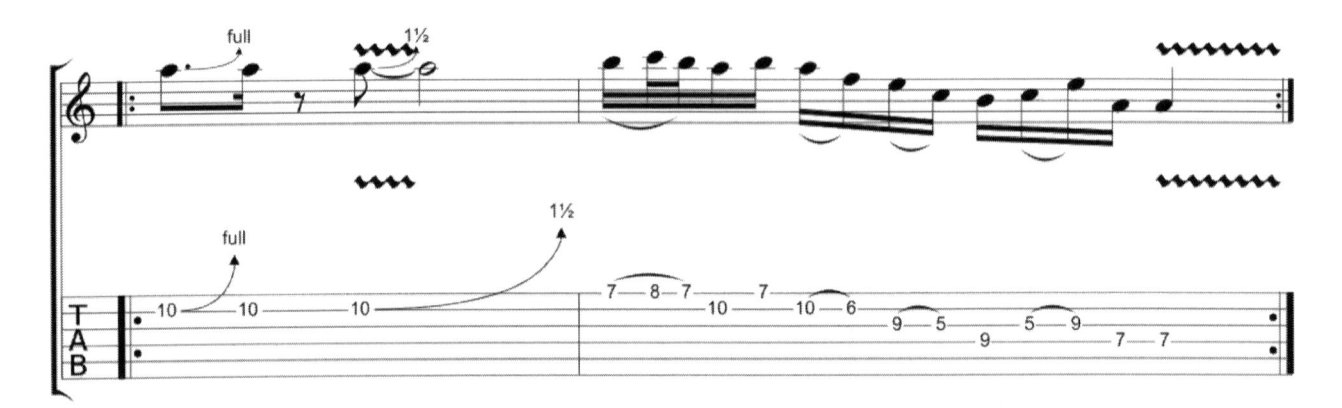

A Hirojoshi Pentatonic – Position 3 'C' Shape

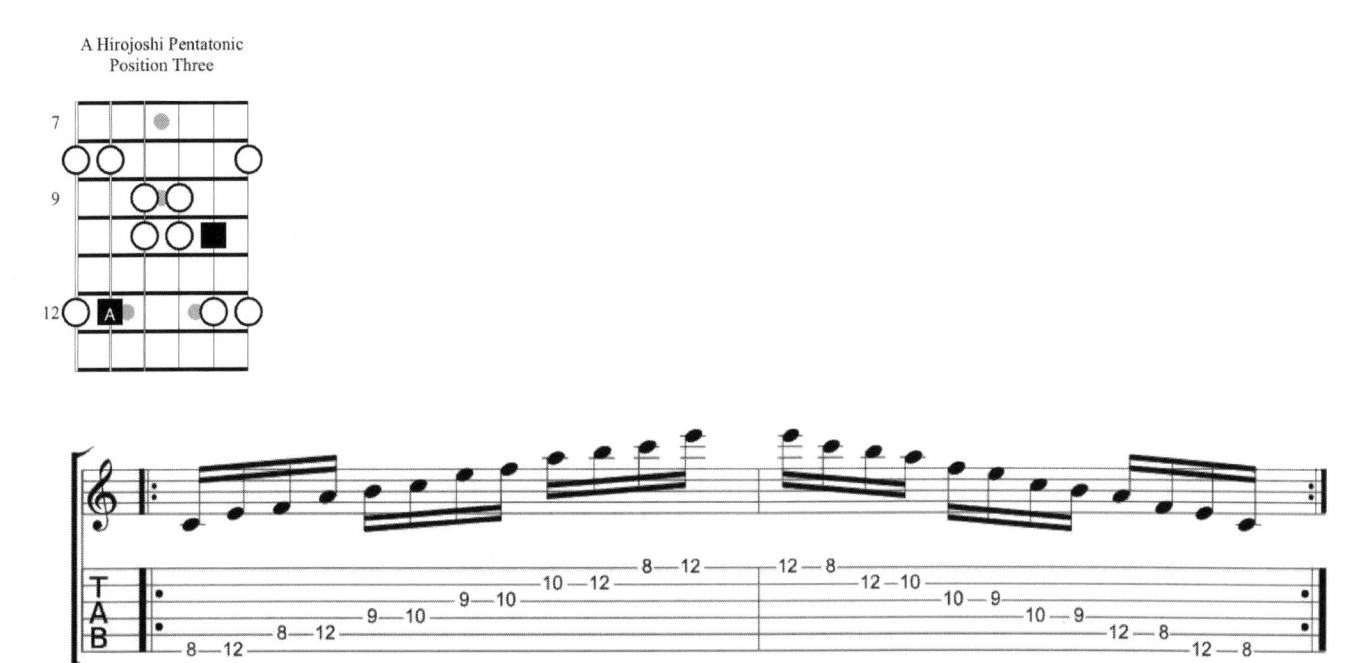

This lick is dark and melancholic. The triads in bar one create tension, and the addition of double-stops add more suspense. The triad is created using the notes A C F and A. This triad is essentially an F major triad with the root note of A. The flutter of legato-based notes at the end of bar two finishes this lick up with a flourish.

Example 13c

A Hirojoshi Pentatonic – Position 4 'A' Shape

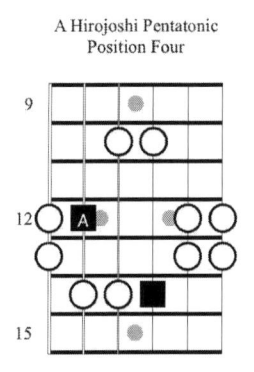

77

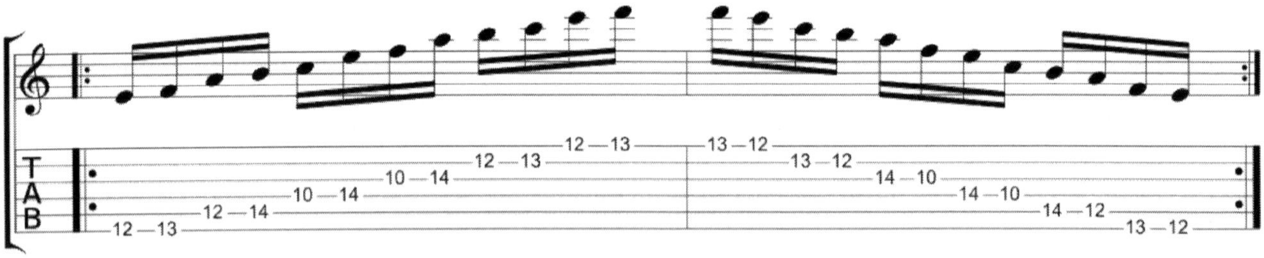

Example 13d is another long, fluid legato line. You can, of course, swap alternate picking for legato, which will make the lick sound quite different although I think that the Hirojoshi Pentatonic really favours hammer-ons and pull-offs.

Example 13d

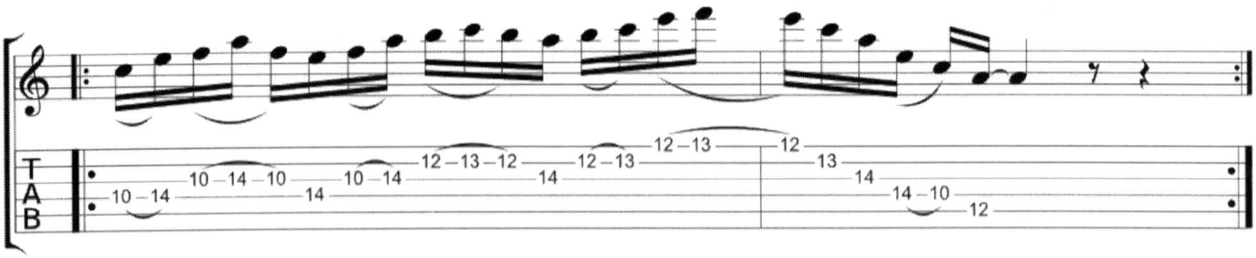

A Hirojoshi Pentatonic – Position 5 'G' Shape

A Hirojoshi Pentatonic
Position Five

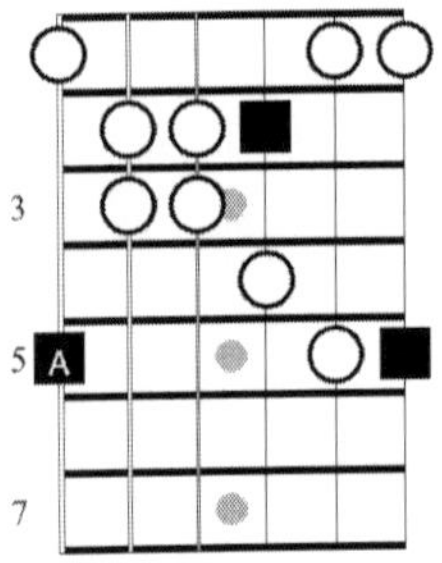

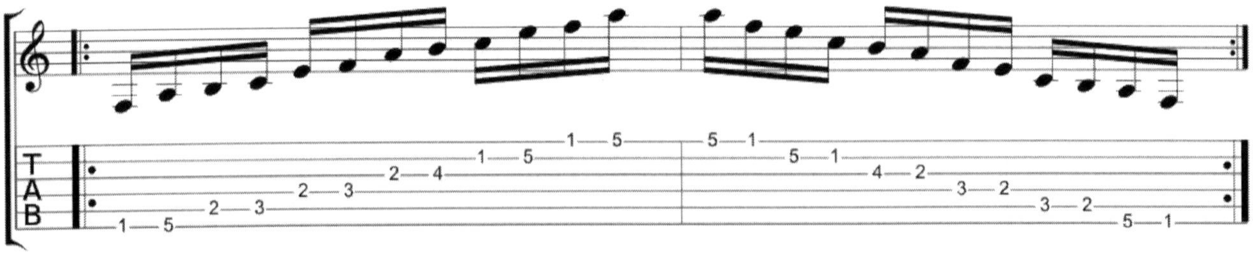

This next idea is a riff created from the Hirojoshi Pentatonic scale which works well when played with heavy distortion. The combination of a simple, single-note line and two chunky power chords set up the sound.

You could try using 'A5' and 'F5' power chords as a backing for all the licks and ideas used in this chapter.

Example 13e

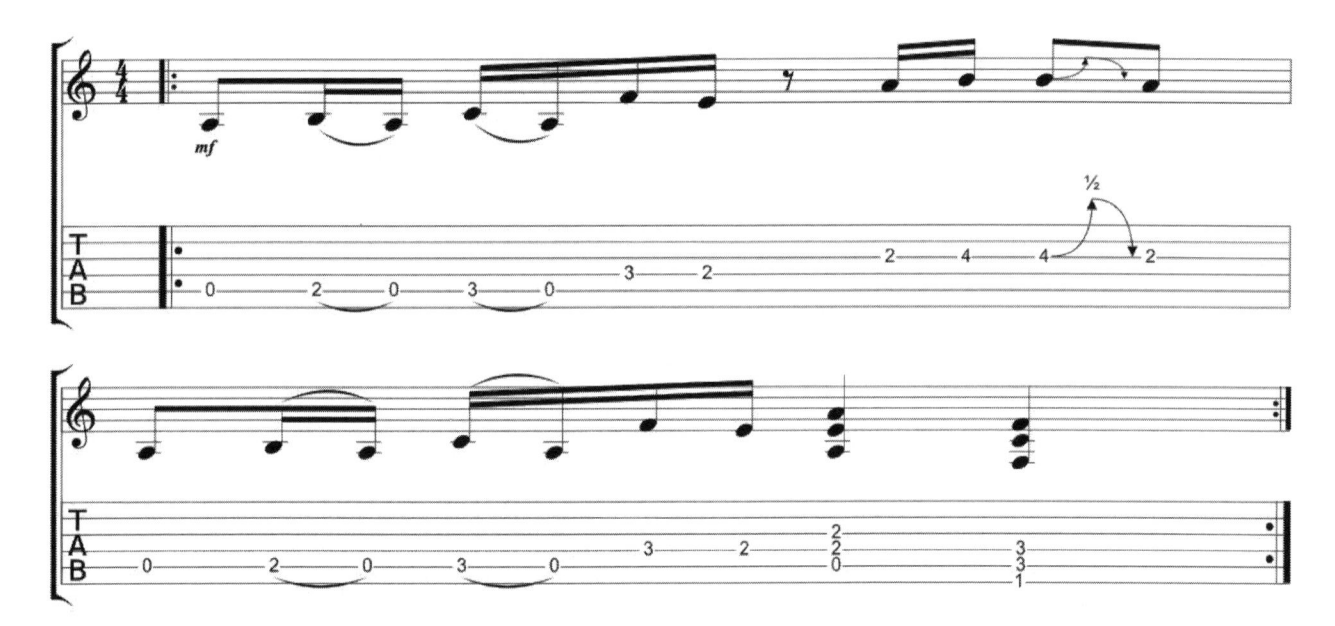

The licks in this chapter once again have an Eastern feel and fit perfectly over Backing Track Six. The dark tones created when soloing using this scale work wonderfully in a modern rock/metal context and really suit bends, hammer-ons, pull-offs, vibrato and slides.

Chapter Fourteen: Improvising

In chapter three I discussed a simple tactic for building solos by combining a lick you have already learnt with improvisation. Shown below are a few more 'road maps' that you can use to create your own solos.

Be sure to keep coming back to licks you already know, they will act as anchor points for your solos. Each lick should be one you are already comfortable with and can play fluently.

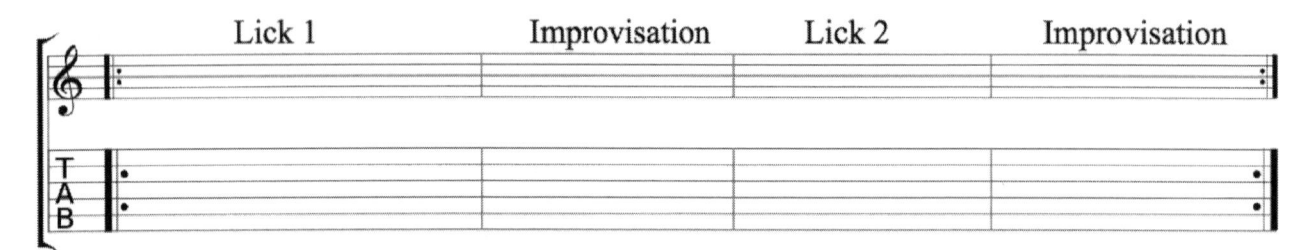

Lick 1	Improvisation	Lick 2	Improvisation

The previous idea can be reversed so that you begin with a short period of improvisation and play a lick afterwards. Try sticking to these formulas when you start improvising with the licks in this book so that your solos will always sound prepared and confident.

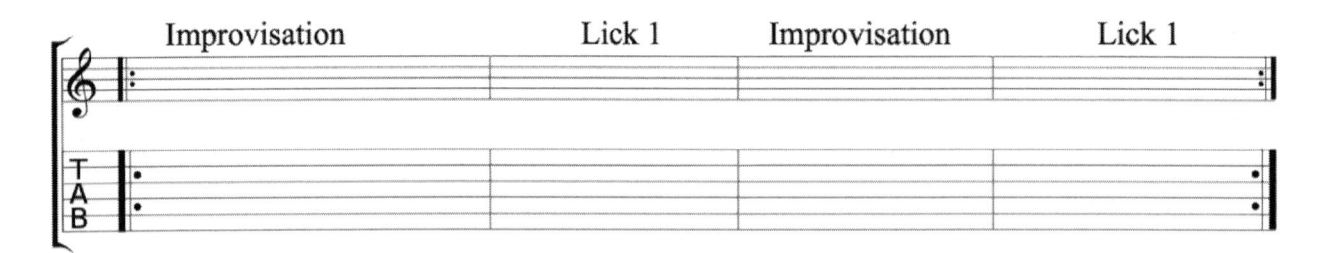

Improvisation	Lick 1	Improvisation	Lick 1

The classic solos that we hear on records are rarely improvised. They are usually constructed ahead of time to fit the track, however, certain elements are often improvised around a structured set of bars like in the previous two examples.

As well as the previous approach of mixing bars of improvisation with prepared licks, another popular method for improving your improvisational skill is to restrict yourself to using only a few notes from a given scale. Forcing yourself to concentrate on new ways to play the notes you have available tackles any fears of approaching full scale shapes when improvising.

Note Restricted Improvisation

Restrict yourself to playing a maximum of four notes on two adjacent strings using just one scale, and see how many ideas you can create. We are going to use the A Minor Pentatonic scale as the basis for these examples, but you can use any pentatonic scale in this book.

Four Notes From A Minor Pentatonic

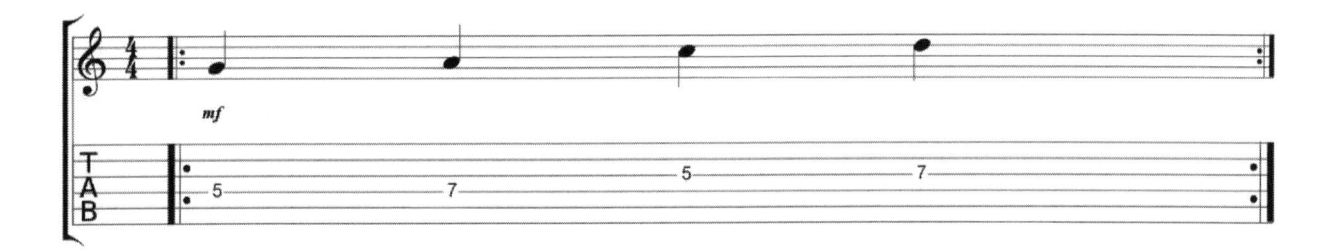

A good starting point is to take only the above four notes from the A Minor Pentatonic scale and using Backing Track One, see how many ideas you can create. After a minute or two you may feel you have run out of ideas. This is normal at first but with practice your creativity will grow.

At first the possibilities seem incredibly limited when dealing with only four notes, but by applying bends, hammer-ons, pull-offs, slides and vibrato the number of melodic options are vast. Shown below are two simple ways to combine these four notes:

The simplest technique you can use is to simply slide between each note. This easy and effective idea is used frequently in blues and rock licks. The four designated notes can be slid in any direction as long as no other notes are added. Treat these ideas as a starting point and try to come up with as many of your own ideas as possible: the more the better.

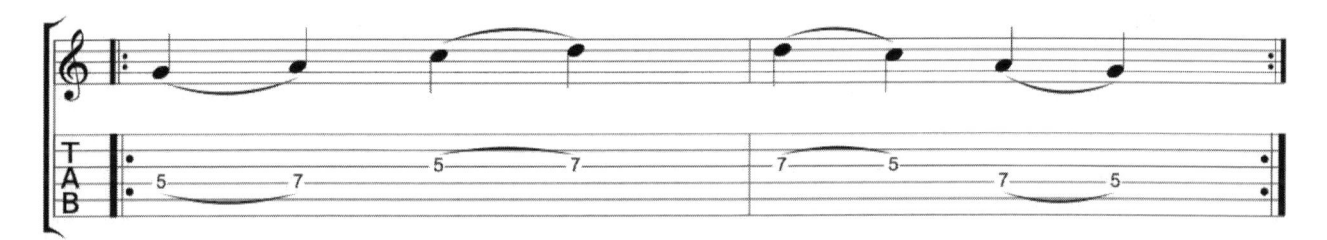

Another idea is to use legato (hammer-ons and pull-offs). As with the sliding example, apply legato in any way you wish, but only use the four notes from the scale.

Vibrato and bends will work better in certain parts of scales than others, so experimentation is crucial to find what appeals to your ear. If you are stuck for ideas, refer to the licks seen throughout the book to see where I added bends in each shape.

After five minutes of restricting yourself to these four notes, begin to explore a different four notes; preferably connected in some way to the original four.

Apply the same principles as before to see how many melodic ideas you can create. For example, you could use the following four notes as an extension of the previous exercise:

Four Notes A Minor Pentatonic

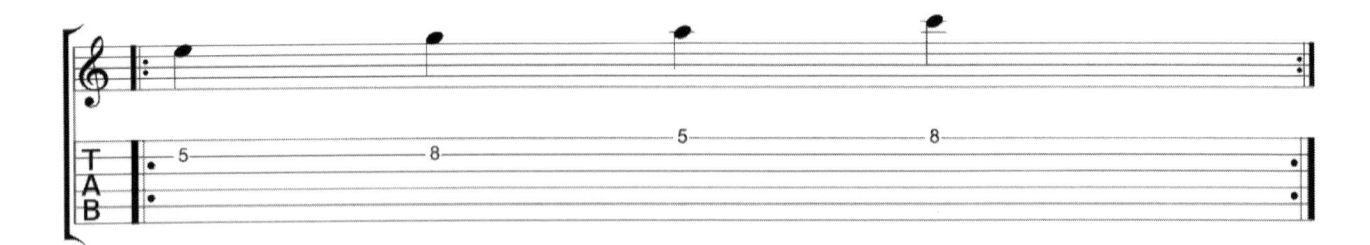

```
Tab:
e|--------------------------------||
B|--------------------------------||
G|--------------------------------||
D|--------------------------------||
A|--5--------8--------5--------8--||
E|--------------------------------||
```

Once again, explore these notes over Backing Track One using the techniques described above.

Next, try doing the same exercise in a different position on the neck to access new sounds and nuances.

Four Notes A Minor Pentatonic Position 2

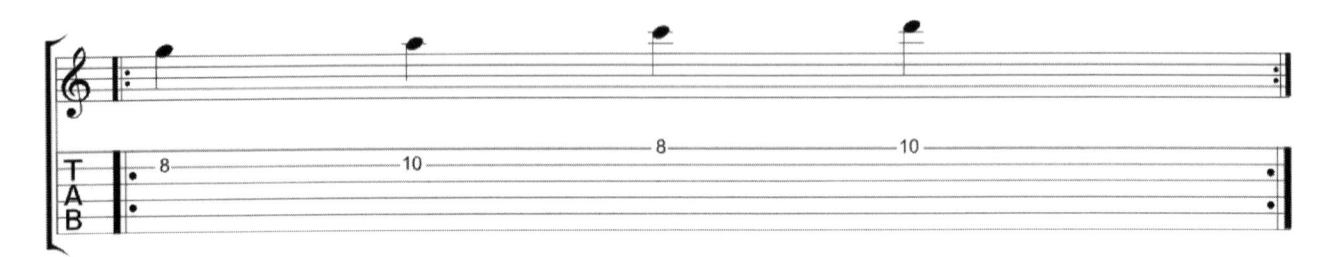

```
Tab:
e|--------------------------------||
B|--------------------------------||
G|--------------------------------||
D|------------------8-------10----||
A|--8--------10-------------------||
E|--------------------------------||
```

Shown above are four notes from the A Minor Pentatonic scale in position two. These four notes have the same fret spacing as the original four notes on the previous page so you can easily transfer your improvisational ideas from one to another.

Once you are comfortable improvising with each individual four-note shape, put on a backing track and restrict yourself to *six* notes and repeat the exercises.

Rhythmic Improvisation

Pick any pentatonic scale and put on the accompanying backing track. Without the guitar, clap or tap out a rhythm over the backing track. Then, with the guitar, create a lick that uses the rhythm you have just created. The notes you play can be located anywhere on the neck. This simple technique forces you to incorporate rhythmic diversity into your lead guitar licks. If you are struggling to remember the rhythms you create, try to record them.

Technique Specific Improvisation

In contrast to *note*-specific improvisation, it is possible to use *technique*-specific improvisation: Pick a pentatonic scale and play the corresponding backing track. Choose one technique (bends, legato, slides or vibrato) and solo with just that one technique. The whole fretboard can be used in this exercise as there are no note restrictions.

Chapter Fifteen: Building Melodic Phrases

Video: www.fundamental-changes.com/exotic-pentatonic-soloing Password: hirojoshi

Now that you understand how the scale shapes and licks from the pentatonic scales work let's take a look at how to build your own riffs and licks.

Tip #1 – How many notes?

Often we use single notes to create musical ideas. One way to get creative is to view a scale shape in terms of two-note intervals, three-note triads, or four-note chord shapes. Examine your favourite scales, and try creating your own licks from these divisions. See how many new ideas you can get from each pentatonic scale shape.

Tip #2 – Add Specialist Techniques

The five techniques that form the core of your soloing arsenal are slides, bends, hammer-ons, pull-offs, and vibrato. Using a mixture of these will instantly add life to any scale ideas. There are no specific rules on when you should add specialist techniques to your playing and often it depends on which genre of music you are playing.

Take a small part of a pentatonic scale (perhaps two or three strings) and play a simple melody. Next, try to introduce some techniques that enhance the melody. This exercise forms the basis of building melodic lines of any length. After you have developed one lick in this manner, try adding another lick to it, using either the same scale shape or another position.

Gradually add more specialist techniques and remember that scale shapes provide the template for your lead playing, but the techniques you add bring them to life.

Tip #3 – Keep your Playing Melodic

As guitarists, we can get lost in a world of flashy technique. Try to keep your core playing something that you can sing. Of course, there may be licks you play that are flashy and more technical but if you keep your main themes melodic they are more likely to be well received than endless 'noodling'.

Tip #4 – Phrasing

Two of my favourite ways to use musical phrasing are to add pauses between your licks and to alter your dynamics (playing louder or quietly). One thing to remember is that 'the plectrum never runs out of breath.' Try singing your licks out loud: where would the melody naturally pause? How loud or soft should it be? Where would you have to breathe?

Another element to consider in your phrasing is to create interesting rhythms. Don't play every note the same length. Include different feels and grooves depending on what you are playing over.

Tip #5 – Repetition with Variation

Repetition with variation is a 'golden rule' when creating longer solos. Try to create a theme you can return to throughout your solo. When you revisit your theme add some subtle changes; these could be as simple as adding one specialist technique. This helps the listener to latch onto the main hook of your solo, and subconsciously feel rewarded when they hear it again. For a great example of this, check out the main theme to Joe Satriani's Surfing with the Alien.

Conclusion

Whether you are a technical wizard or prefer simpler licks, anyone can benefit from evaluating their approach to playing melodies on the guitar. Try to emulate your favourite solos: think about what makes them sound so special.

Chapter Sixteen: Minor Pentatonic Substitution

A common technique that is used with pentatonic scales is called *substitution*. Pentatonic substitution is taking one scale (for example, the Minor Pentatonic scale), and playing it over different chords to create new and exciting flavours.

The Minor Pentatonic scale, as we saw in chapter three, fits perfectly over a minor chord. The intervals in the scale are 1 b3 4 5 b7. What is exciting is that if we move the Minor Pentatonic scale shape but still play it over the same underlying chord, we can access new intervals with no extra effort.

This chapter touches on a few useful ways to use pentatonic substitution.

The 'Eric Johnson' Trick– Superimposed Minor Pentatonic from the 5th

My favourite way to apply pentatonic substitution is using an idea I stole from Eric Johnson.

The A Minor Pentatonic scale contains the notes of A, C, D, E and G. Over an A root note this gives the intervals of 1 b3 4 5 b7. However, it is possible to play other pentatonic scales over an A minor chord.

The 'E' Minor Pentatonic contains the notes of E, G, A, B and D.

Playing the E Minor Pentatonic scale *over* a root note of A creates the intervals: 5 b7 1 2 4. These intervals are almost identical to the ones in the A Minor Pentatonic scale; the only difference is that the b3 in the A Minor Pentatonic scale has been replaced by a 2nd.

These intervals (1, 2, 4, 5 and b7) sound great when played over an A minor chord but as the b3 has been dropped, the sound created is slightly ambiguous.

Rule: Play a Minor Pentatonic from a 5th above the root.

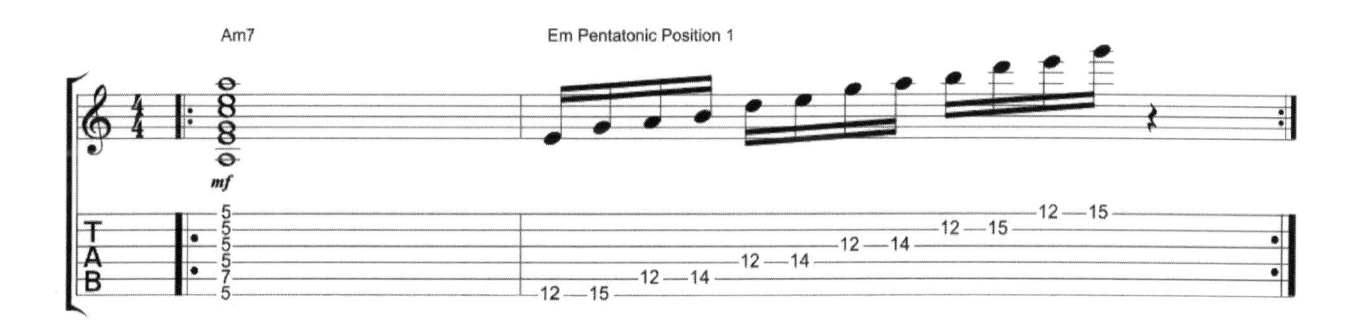

The 'Dorian' Trick – Superimposed Minor Pentatonic from the 2nd

In this example, the B Minor Pentatonic scale 'B D E F# A,' is played over a root note of A. This imposes the intervals of 2, 4, 5, 6, and 1. By playing the Minor Pentatonic scale two frets above the root of the underlying minor chord we can create a Dorian flavour by introducing the natural 6th interval.

Rule: Play a Minor Pentatonic on the 2nd above the root.

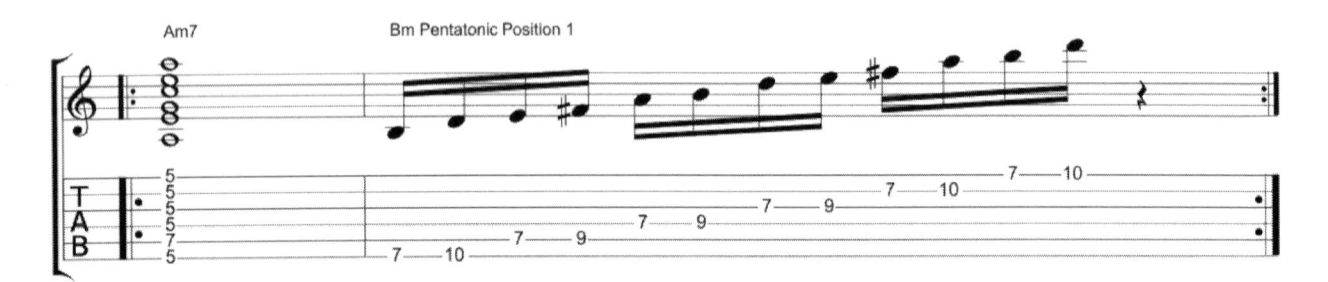

The 'Lydian' Trick – Superimposed Minor Pentatonic from the 7th

The sound of the Lydian scale can be created using a Minor Pentatonic scale. In this example, the notes of a G# Minor Pentatonic scale are played over an A root note. This imposes the intervals of 7, 2, 3, #4, and 6. By playing a Minor Pentatonic scale one fret below the root of a Major chord (or Major7#11) chord, the #4th interval is added.

Rule: Play a Minor Pentatonic on the 7th above (a semitone below) the root.

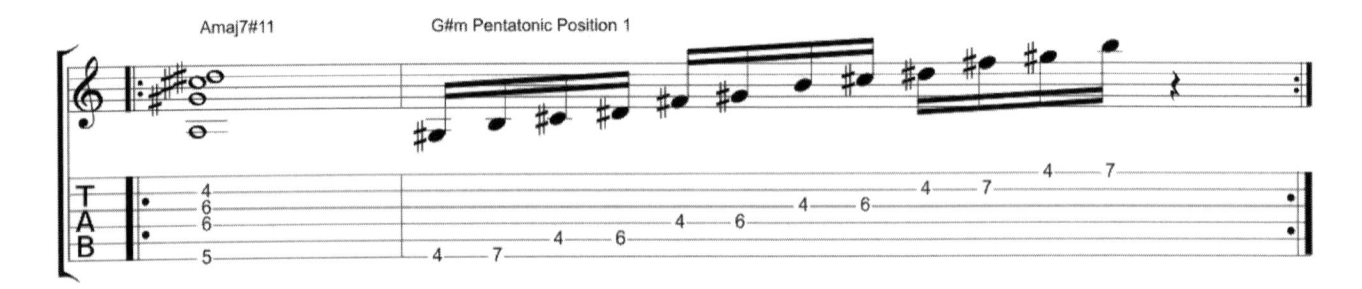

The 'Natural Minor' Trick – Superimposed Minor Pentatonic from the 4th

The Aeolian or Natural Minor scale is one of the most common minor scales in Western music. It has a long-standing relationship with classic rock but was also frequently heard in classical music. The standout interval is the b6 which has a tension that wants to resolve down to the 5th.

The sound of the Aeolian scale can be created using a Minor Pentatonic scale substitution. In this example, we will play the notes of a D Minor Pentatonic scale over an A root note. This creates us the intervals of 4, b6, b7, 1 and b3. By playing the Minor Pentatonic from the 4th of A, it is possible to create an Aeolian sound.

Rule: Play a Minor Pentatonic from the 4th above the root.

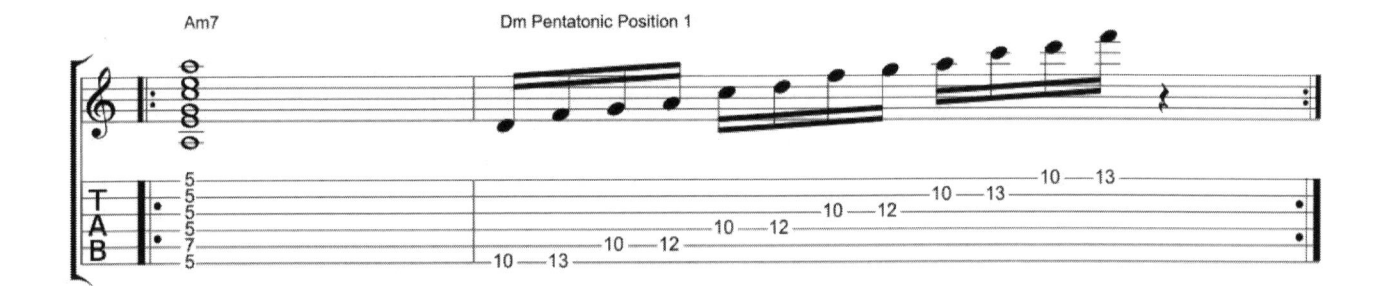

The 'Altered Dominant' Trick – Superimposed Minor Pentatonic from the b3rd

Playing over jazz chords is often a challenge, especially for traditional blues-rock players. This example creates a jazzy, sophisticated sound using only a Minor Pentatonic scale. For this trick a C Minor Pentatonic scale is played over an A root note to impose the intervals of #9, b5, #5, b7, and b9.' This substitution gives us access to common alterations that are played over altered dominant chords, such as A7#5 or A7b9. This scale substitution is an easy way to sound complex and knowledgeable when playing over altered dominant chords. Just make sure you resolve your lines cleanly.

Rule: Play a Minor Pentatonic from the b3rd above the root.

This has been a very brief introduction to the fascinating world of pentatonic substitutions. Although there is a myriad of other pentatonic substitution options, the ones shown here are created using only Minor Pentatonic scales.

Some of the substitutions are easier on the ear than others so always be aware what the root note of the underlying chord is, and make sure to always resolve to a strong chord tone.

Chapter Seventeen: Developing your Sound

This book has covered a wealth of scales and licks across a wide range of musical genres. From classic rock through to Japanese folk, exotic pentatonic scales are incredibly versatile.

Once you have learnt a few exotic scales and mastered some licks, it's time to put them together into a complete musical package.

The following points will show you how to turn scalic notes, patterns and licks into real music by developing your own tone and sound.

The Player

The single most important aspect of tone production is the person playing the guitar. Most professional guitarists can make any instrument or amp sound great. You are the source of tone! The first thing to do is to make sure that *every* note you play has meaning and purpose. Jeff Beck has recorded some of the best guitar playing on the planet, and he has said, "Better to play one note well, than a thousand notes badly." Blow by Blow and Guitar Shop are some of Jeff Beck's finest works and come highly recommended.

The Guitar

There is no specific guitar that suits playing pentatonic scales more than any other, although there are some classics, you could consider. Arguably the Fender Stratocaster, the Fender Telecaster and the Gibson Les Paul are the most commonly used instruments in modern electric guitar playing.

Get to know your instrument! Every instrument has subtle nuances that make it unique. Get to know how your volume, tone, and pickup selector controls subtly shape your sound.

Paul Gilbert uses the volume pot to control his tone. He creates clean sounds with the volume pot low, at around two or three, his medium crunch sounds at around five or six and his rip-roaring solo sound with the volume control turned to nine or ten. Using this technique he can play a whole track just by adjusting the volume controls. This technique is incredibly versatile if you don't have hundreds of pedals but do have a nice amp sound.

The pickup selector gives you control over the tone your guitar produces. The pickup nearest the bridge will have the brightest, harshest tone and is often used for solos. The pickups get progressively warmer and smoother as you move towards the neck pickup. Often, people only use two of the five possible pickup selector positions, preferring the warm neck pickup for rhythm and the bridge pickup for solos and riffs. However, you should experiment with all the pickup selection options you have available. Don't be afraid to break convention.

There are two main types of pickups; single-coil and humbucker. Single-coil pickups have a classic, clear tone. They are highly dynamic and favour clean to moderate distortion settings. Humbucking pickups are warmer and fatter sounding and are often used in heavy rock, metal and jazz.

One misconception is that spending a lot of money will guarantee you an amazing instrument. My advice is to buy the best possible instrument you can afford and learn it inside out. Often buying a second-hand guitar allows you to get twice the guitar for half the money. Look online and ask your friends to see what's available. Read reviews and be search out the types of guitars used in the music you like.

The Amp

Throughout the years Marshall, Fender and Vox have been the most popular manufacturers and have provided industry standard tones at affordable prices. Classic amplifiers from these manufacturers include the:

Fender Champ
Fender Blackface
Fender Princeton
Fender Deluxe
Vox AC30
Marshall JCM 800

These days there are an enormous range of amplifiers available so choosing one comes down to individual tastes and preference.

The amplifier controls that sculpt your sound are the gain and EQ controls. Although adjusting the gain control will have an effect on the overall volume, think of it as a tone control, not a volume control. Adjusting the gain increases or decreases the amount of distortion heard in the amplifier. Tone creation is very personal, and subjective so listen to many different guitarists and decide on what you want to hear as a 'ballpark' idea, then shape the sound to your own preference.

The bass, middle and treble EQ controls on the amplifier are the main tone sculptors and allow you to mould the guitar sound to your desired tone. If you are in doubt set your amplifier's EQ to six, five, six (bass, middle and treble.) This is a good starting point to build from and normally works when testing out a new amplifier.

Pedals

Building a pedal board, or creating unique tones from a multi-fx unit can be a lengthy, on-going process. My advice before you buy lots of fancy new gear is to make sure you know any gear you already have inside out. When I started playing guitar, I didn't have the money to buy lots of gadgets. That forced me to know my amplifier inside out, a skill I still use to this day. Make sure to read reviews, watch YouTube videos and, of course, play every pedal yourself to see which ones enhance your musical style.

Strings

The most important thing to do before any recording or live session is to re-string your guitar, (I like to have had the strings on for about a day to let them settle in.) Brand new strings make an incredible difference to the overall tone of the guitar; I am always amazed at how lifeless and dull strings can get even after a week's playing.

The lighter the strings, the easier they are to play. Heavier strings have a fatter, warmer tone, but techniques such as bending can be more challenging. I recommend you try different string gauges and manufacturers until your find a set that works for you. For the recordings in this book I used Ernie Ball Super Slinky strings with a gauge of 9-42.

Pick or Fingers?

One of the biggest factors in tone production is how you hit the strings. The thickness of your pick/plectrum will impact your tone. The thicker the pick, the bolder and fuller the sound whereas thinner picks usually produce a sparkly clear tone. I personally use 'Jim Dunlop Jazz 3' plectrums. This is the one area of my playing that has not changed throughout the years. I find the control I get from these picks, especially when alternate picking boosts my confidence and control tremendously.

"Picks are for fairies!" is another inspiring quote from tone-master Jeff Beck. He is referring to the fact that you can get incredible control and touch by playing every note with your fingers. Most people only associate finger-picking with rhythm and chord work, but finger-picked lead guitar can be some of the most emotive and creative. *Put down your plectrum and play your favourite lead lines with your fingers.* It is also possible to use hybrid picking to access to both finger-picking and pick at the same time.

My Gear

While filming and recording the audio for this book this video book I used one guitar, one amplifier and one microphone. I used my Fender Texas Special Fat Stratocaster into my Fender Super Champ X2 amplifier. I captured the recordings using a Shure SM57 microphone placed close to the amp's grill. As this amp has multiple sounds available I was able to easily capture all the tones I needed.

Playing with Other Musicians

By now, you have learnt licks, created fun and inspiring improvisations and developed your tone. By working with other musicians and seeing how they create music, you will develop a better idea of how to create your own tone and style. Ask the musicians you are working with to give you constructive feedback about your tone, and to give you ideas they may have to improve it.

Music is to be played, and there is no better feeling than jamming! My top tip for jamming with other musicians is 'play with people who are better than you'. Working with musicians more technically and musically advanced will inspire you. Learning to read music notation, and having a good grasp of modern music theory can help you to interact with other musicians.

If you can't play with other musicians why not invest in a looper pedal (such as a TC Electronic 'Ditto') to play with more of a live feel?.

Conclusion

The goal of this book is to inspire new and exciting directions in your lead guitar playing. It is easy as a guitarist to sometimes feel stuck with the same scale shapes and licks. The truth is, sometimes all you need to do is adapt just one note to create a new sound. You can also add different rhythmic grooves, specialist techniques, and jam with other musicians.

Build your own pentatonic scales! All you need to remember is that there must be five different notes in each scale. Most of the time it will be worth having a root note, although as proven in the 'No Root add9' Pentatonic chapter, that isn't essential.

Once you have picked five notes that you enjoy the sound of, map them out across the fretboard. Become very familiar with one shape first before starting to learn all five shapes. This will help to cement the sound of the scale in your head. Practice the scale using all the ways you learnt in the Chapter One.

After you become familiar with the new pentatonic shape, let the fun commence! Write and document as many licks as you can, either as video, audio or tablature for a later date.

I hope that the information in this book helps you to explore fresh new ideas in your guitar playing. Make sure that you study the videos on www.fundamantal-changes.com and download the audio to get the most out of this book.

Recommended Listening

The Jimi Hendrix Experience – Electric Ladyland
Eric Clapton – Slowhand
BB King – Riding With The King (with Eric Clapton)
Carlos Santana – Ultimate Santana
Albert King – Born Under A Bad Sign
Chuck Berry – Johnny B. Goode
Freddie King – Hide Away: The Best Of Freddie King
Stevie Ray Vaughan – Texas Flood
Jeff Beck – Performing This Week
Pink Floyd – Dark Side Of The Moon
John Mayer – Continuum
Gary Moore – Still Got The Blues
Led Zeppelin – I, II and IV: Remastered
The Allman Brothers Band: Brothers and Sisters (Super Deluxe Edition)
Joe Bonamassa - Dust Bowl
Kenny Burrell - Midnight Blue Remastered
Robben Ford – Talk To Your Daughter
Larry Carlton: Greatest Hits
Scott Henderson – Tore Down House
Eric Johnson - Ah Via Musicom
Red Hot Chili Peppers – Stadium Arcadium
Joe Satriani – The Essential Joe Satriani
AC/DC - Back in Black
Van Halen – Van Halen
Gun's N Roses – Appetite for Destruction
The Eagles – Hotel California
Deep Purple – Machine Head
Ozzy Osbourne – Blizzard Of Ozz (Expanded Edition)
Metallica – Master Of Puppets
Yes - The Very Best Of
Guthrie Govan – Erotic Cakes
Racer X – Technical Difficulties
Extreme - Pornograffiti
Marty Friedman – Inferno
John Mclaughlin – Greatest Hits
Derek Trucks – The Derek Trucks Band

Other Books from Fundamental Changes

Rock Rhythm Guitar Playing

Heavy Metal Rhythm Guitar

Heavy Metal Lead Guitar Book 1

Heavy Metal Lead Guitar Book 2

The Practical Guide to Modern Music Theory for Guitarists

Rock Guitar Un-CAGED: The CAGED System and 100 Licks for Rock Guitar

Guitar Fretboard Fluency

Guitar Scales in Context

Complete Technique for Modern Guitar

The CAGED System and 100 Licks for Blues Guitar

The Complete Guide to Playing Blues Guitar Book One: Rhythm Guitar

The Complete Guide to Playing Blues Guitar Book Two: Melodic Phrasing

The Complete Guide to Playing Blues Guitar Book Three: Beyond Pentatonics

The Complete Guide to Playing Blues Guitar Compilation

Fundamental Changes in Jazz Guitar: The Major ii V I

Minor ii V Mastery for Jazz Guitar

Jazz Blues Soloing for Guitar

Guitar Chords in Context Part One

Jazz Guitar Chord Mastery (Guitar Chords in Context Part Two)

Funk Guitar Mastery

The Complete Technique, Theory and Scales Compilation for Guitar

Sight Reading Mastery for Guitar

Beginner's Guitar Lessons: The Essential Guide

Chord Tone Soloing for Jazz Guitar

Facebook: FundamentalChangesInGuitar

@sdpguitar

Printed in Great Britain
by Amazon